HEALING EMOTIONAL TRAUMA

PRACTICAL PATHWAYS TO DECREASE ANXIETY, ANGER & LOWER BLOOD PRESSURE

JAYAN MARIE LANDRY PHD

LEARN THIS GROUNDBREAKING SOUND THERAPY
TECHNIQUE: THE LANDRY METHOD©

BALBOA.
PRESS
A DIVISION OF HAY HOUSE

Balboa Press books may be ordered through booksellers or by contacting:

Balboa Press
A Division of Hay House
1663 Liberty Drive
Bloomington, IN 47403
www.balboapress.com
1 (877) 407-4847

Because of the dynamic nature of the Internet, any web addresses or
links contained in this book may have changed since publication and
may no longer be valid. The views expressed in this work are solely those
of the author and do not necessarily reflect the views of the publisher,
and the publisher hereby disclaims any responsibility for them.

The author of this book does not dispense medical advice or prescribe the use
of any technique as a form of treatment for physical, emotional, or medical
problems without the advice of a physician, either directly or indirectly. The
intent of the author is only to offer information of a general nature to help
you in your quest for emotional and spiritual well-being. In the event you use
any of the information in this book for yourself, which is your constitutional
right, the author and the publisher assume no responsibility for your actions.

Any people depicted in stock imagery provided by Thinkstock are
models, and such images are being used for illustrative purposes only.
Certain stock imagery © Thinkstock.

Print information available on the last page.

ISBN: 978-1-5043-3628-4 (sc)
ISBN: 978-1-5043-3630-7 (hc)
ISBN: 978-1-5043-3629-1 (e)

Library of Congress Control Number: 2015911534

Balboa Press rev. date: 10/22/2015

CONTENTS

List of Tables in the order of appearance in body of text

List of Figures

FOREWORD

When seeing clients in my private psychotherapy practice, I glance toward the sofa end table where a treasured gift keeps track of session time. On the opposite side of this special clock a brass plaque is engraved with the inscription:

And how old will you be if you don't ...

In my late forties, divorced after a twenty-four year marriage, I was sitting with my close friend Ruthie on my living room couch. While contemplating the future, I asked the proverbial rhetorical question, "What will I do with my life now?" Ruthie said, "What have you always wanted to do but didn't have the energy or time?" I responded, "I always wanted to get my doctorate in counseling psychology; however, it will take five years and I'll be fifty-two." With deep wisdom and a voice filled with conviction, Ruthie—who would give me the engraved graduation clock five years later—looked squarely into my eyes and countered, "And how old will you be in five years if you don't get it?" The obvious answer was fifty-two because time would march on either way. Transforming the hypothetical question into reality, I earned the worthwhile degree by fifty-two. Never underestimate the power of words from a wise and loving friend. For just when you feel the threads of confusion unraveling your life as it's coming apart, a friend offers clarity and helps you gather the pieces. Weaving them into a new cohesive and beautiful pattern is entirely up to you.

Back to School

I returned to school for my doctorate after decades of clinical practice in nursing and mental health. After the first three years and 120 credits, I entered the much-dreaded phase two of the postgraduate degree program. Charged with the task of creating and executing an original research project, I needed to choose my study topic. How would I contribute to the body of knowledge already gained from preexisting research in the field of psychology and mental well-being? After months of trying to come up with the answer, one morning it appeared as I looked no further than my refrigerator door and saw Brenda's magnet.

Brenda Waller was a devoted wife, mother, sister, daughter, aunt, neighbor, registered nurse, Trauma Intervention Program of Merrimack Valley, Inc. (TIP) volunteer, and one of my dearest friends. She was also one of my greatest mentors, teaching me about life and death from my seat in the front row of her life challenges. She was a role model for unconditional love, loyalty, and devotion. Family and friends had the privilege of experiencing the healing power of her strong will, positive attitude, and love of nature as we joined to fight the battle with cancer that took her life far too soon at 3:58 P.M. on November 4, 2006. The magnet was one of the few material possessions she left behind as an earthly reminder of a treasured union during our relationship journey. The inscription, found in Joseph Campbell's *The Hero's Journey* (1990) read:

> "Follow your bliss, and doors will open
> where you would not have expected."[1]

Reading this snapshot of Campbell's philosophy planted a seed in my subconscious, and soon that seed would manifest into the next door I needed to open on my road to higher education.

Spirituality

Throughout my life, being a *thinker* was my natural default. When faced with challenges, I attempted to "figure it out" by reading this or that book. For most situations, this approach offered me answers and the security needed to cope with just about everything in my world. I got some of it right, and many times the books were helpful, but eventually I came to realize that not all understanding was so easily explained.

I honor my mother for the many ways she showed her love to us. I am also at peace knowing she made decisions within the best of her ability, based on her life experiences. Her love and parental instruction included consistently bringing my younger brother and me to church each week for confession on Saturdays and Mass on Sundays. We learned about sin and forgiveness, right and wrong, through our mysterious and loving God.

At the majestic St. Leo's Church, on Saturday evenings, I waited for my turn to pull back the heavy purple velvet curtain in the private confessional booth. With trepidation I entered, knelt down and humbly rested my forehead onto my folded hands. Even though this was a weekly ritual, I was always startled by the sound created when the priest slid back the solid screen with one quick motion. He was on the other side of the barrier, and remained hidden behind the veiled, honeycombed hedge that smelled like a mix of sweat and plastic. With a heart for reconciliation, it was my cue to share personal sins and transgressions with the cloaked, unrevealed holy man. I both feared and imagined him being upset or bored with me as I repeated, "Bless me Father, for I have sinned. This week I took the Lord's name in vain three times and didn't get along with my annoying younger brother."

The penance that followed as I exited the booth and knelt down on the marble church altar was pretty much the same, three Our Fathers and two Hail Marys. This exercise taught me to be accountable for my actions in relationship to God's expectations. Feeling purged and clean, we went home and had our favorite meal-hot dogs, beans, and my mother's homemade piccalilli fresh from our garden's bounty. On Sunday mornings we rose and went to church with our mother. Although often bored during parts of Mass, combined with Saturday confession, I was grateful for this important exposure to God and Jesus, which facilitated the birth of my spiritual journey.

Throughout the years that followed, I continued to develop my relationship with God by speaking and listening to Him frequently, on my own and in communion with others. As an adult, seeking to expand faith, spirit, and mindfulness, I've been blessed with a number of life-changing opportunities derived from travel and retreat participation on my own and with family and friends.

My former husband and I were touched and overwhelmed by the humility, faith, and respect from the wonderful people of Bali, Indonesia. With the majority of Bali's population adhering to Hinduism, they have over 20,000 temples and shrines known as the "Island of the Gods." On arrival night, from our balcony, we saw the ocean scattered with lit candles floating on one-time use handmade grass mats. The purpose of the annual ceremony was to seek favor from the Gods of education for each Balinese child. Three times, every day, hotel staff quietly offered fruit and flower sacrifices on those mats, into our bungalow temple as they prayed for the success of our island visit. The peaceful God loving respectful Balinese people genuinely cared for us, wasted nothing, and honored their Gods with personal sacrifice. When I arrived home, for a few months that followed, I had an almost "allergic" reaction to the stimulating noise, wastefulness and disregard of God by many in our culture.

With the support of skilled staff at Miraval Resort and Spa, in the Tucson, Arizona desert, my brother and I learned about transitions, letting go, conquering fear and compromise during our Quantum Leap II. We were challenged to explore new ways of communicating while each of us climbed up the same 35-foot pole. Arriving at the top, we discovered the hardest part was hoisting our bodies onto a small cookie sheet-sized platform without any leverage. Gratefully he arrived first and offered down one hand as he guided me to stand next to him. Together we found balance while the pole swayed deeply in the wind. Each of us decided what needed to be left behind, and while holding hands we jumped off into the unknown. Once safely on the ground, I experienced a temporary overwhelming adrenaline rush followed by a renewed faith and self-confidence that has never dissipated.

On the East Coast of the United States, at the Berkshire Mountain foothills, Lenox, Massachusetts is home to the Kripalu Center for Yoga and Health. Personal retreats at the center were critical in the early stages of healing post-divorce, and continue to be an annual respite for self-renewal. One weekend, program leaders were discussing the power of the unseen and unexplainable in the world. Headed outside with my lunch tray to enjoy the breathtaking Berkshires, I passed a hallway poster that caught my eye. It contained a quote by Albert Einstein, one of the world's greatest thinkers:

> The most beautiful thing we can experience is the mysterious. He to whom this emotion is a stranger, who can no longer pause to wonder and stand rapt in awe, is as good as dead: his eyes are closed.[2]

On this particular retreat with birth and rebirth as the theme, I was challenged to stop using *thinking* as my default. Here, I was asked to put aside my familiar pattern of trying to figure out my world using books and mind, and rather *experience* life with body and soul. Clearly this task was outside my comfort zone, but retreats are famous for prodding us to choose new paths of awareness and behaviors. Kripalu leaders along with Albert Einstein were offering me this opportunity to expand my personal perspective. I decided to accept the challenge and submit my will.

The afternoon assignment required group members to *be* with nature and find the mysterious. Having no idea how to accomplish this seemingly herculean task, I began the solo journey on the quiet tree-lined path, cut through the woods, and ended up at the lake. I felt confusion mixed with excitement but breathed into focusing on each step. Arriving lakeside, I embraced the tranquil setting with my eyes and heart, then followed the program leader's instructions. Anxiety amplified as I tucked pen, journal, and study books into my backpack and placed it under a lawn chair. I heard the leader's voice in my head: "Just notice the emotions, and keep deep breathing through it." *Good advice for most things in life.*

My inhalations were getting shorter as my heart beat harder in my chest. Suddenly, feeling like a non-swimmer without water wings in the deep end of the pool, the pounding reached into my eardrums. The thought of not properly documenting this moment in time, coupled with no access to my thinking tools, created a feeling of *uneasiness* for I'd lived my whole life trying *not* to miss vitally important things!

But I continued, stretching beyond my comfortable pattern of behavior, and removed my sandals. I noticed the pleasing sensation of the warm sand squishing up through my toes, offering a gentle massage to the soles of my feet. Feeling calmer, I entered the water, as the cool wetness refreshed my ankles, hot from the hike path. Nudged by an inner voice to tune inward, peacefulness washed over me as the gentle waves caressed my calves. While experiencing these universal gifts, my sensations of sight, sound, smell, touch, and taste were enhanced. Then the mysterious miracle (that might have even impressed Einstein) occurred.

At the water's edge, a large, black, female horned pout (catfish) swam uncomfortably close to my left foot. Its skin was smooth, sleek, almost humanlike, and it sported a long mustache with scattered whiskers. At my feet were thousands of tiny black dots that formed a line behind this momma pout. She seemed to pause slightly as if allowing me just enough time to take in this marvelous surprise of nature. The never-ending black Magic Marker line trailed behind her in the shallow water. This surreal image, coupled with instantaneous confusion, disallowed my mind to register what my eyes were witnessing. Like surrendering to an energy-zapping riptide, I relaxed into the miracle and just *experienced*, without understanding. I had been touched by the mysterious, feeling deeply there would be more to the story.

Of course later, I defaulted to thinking again when my brain came back online. I read up on horned pout and began asking myself questions: Was this a live birth of thousands of new baby horned pouts? Had Momma Pout laid the eggs somewhere else and was taking the embryos out for a swim in the warmth of shallow waters? Apparently this particular kind of fish (which, ironically, my brother Joe and I caught and ate as children) is the only one that contains a Sylvian fissure on its brain's gray matter. This combination of fissure and gray matter offers a spirit of understanding while making no complaints. This was obvious, for they were easy to catch, swallowing entire hooks and then lying quietly in the boat until properly dressed for dinner.

I was experiencing the theme of our Kripalu weekend, birth and rebirth, firsthand, and only by trusting the process could I have received the blessings. Later I'd realize that if I had chosen my usual pattern—sitting on the lawn chair to read and write in an attempt to figure it all out, I would have missed the miracle. Einstein was absolutely correct, and I was "rapt in awe." As I walked back through the woods, up the hill, and into our classroom, I felt a powerful change stirring inside. I couldn't understand this shift but chose to just *feel*. Feel the joy, excitement, anxiety, love, peace, and wonder of it all, mixed into the confusion of not knowing. This is often how life is. Moving forward, I would strive for harmony between books and experience in everyday life, intentionally using all five senses while watching birds at the feeder or when balancing a headstand on my stand up paddle board (SUP). Leaning into the disposition of a horned pout, I developed a spirit of understanding while making no complaints.

During that same afternoon, while lying on the classroom floor practicing a rapid breathing technique, I was blessed with another surreal experience. For what felt like an eternity (probably twenty minutes), I traveled to another place. There, engulfed with indescribable joy, I rebirthed my only child through an inner mind's perspective. With horned-pout birth fresh in my cells, my body recognized an earlier emotional state from my daughter's birth years before. On the floor at Kripalu, I was swaddled with delight and wonder as tears of elation streamed down my face. Unknowingly, there was more joy for me, but it went into circumstantial lockdown on that miraculous occasion years before. Only by opening myself up to the unexplainable was I able to release and then allow the organic flow of nature to give me access to *all* the joy from my daughter's birth, through a personal understanding meant only for me.

As I embark upon middle age, wisdom through experience has offered the gift of embracing the mysterious, with a deeper understanding that all answers are *not* found in books. More likely they are found within each of us, and for me, where God resides. If I can get out of my own way long enough, I will hear the gentle whisperings of my heart and soul's desire (bliss), along with God's will for my life. Adding this concept to my well-entrenched heady style offers me a more effective approach while experiencing my journey here on earth.

There are times that require "head" work, such as phase-two research of a doctoral study. So choosing a blissful study topic would provide the passion and fuel needed to propel me toward mission completion. I tuned inward again to consult my heart and soul in an effort to find my bliss-joy, happiness, paradise, heaven.

Circles of Wisdom

What do I love doing? What actions bring me joy and happiness? What feels like paradise and heaven on earth? What does my soul resonate with? These questions were running through my mind as I entered our local Andover bookstore, Circles of Wisdom. Mitch Nur, an authority on sacred sound instruments, was in town, and I registered for an hour-long Himalayan singing bowl (HSB) session. Hearing about his four decades of academic and experiential workshops on the therapeutic nature of sound, I needed to check out what he had to offer. As founder of the Harmonic Therapy Association and assistant to visiting Tibetan Lamas, he offered numerous master classes on Himalayan singing bowls, gongs, and the Bonpo Shang (flat metal hand bell). I approached Mitch with an open heart and mind, along with some healthy skepticism.

I reclined on a portable padded table in a private room at the bookstore. From head to toe, I was surrounded by bowls and gongs of various sizes, many of which Mitch brought back from the Himalayas. As I lay comfortably with eyes closed, he began to play them, using diverse patterns and intensities. My entire body absorbed the tones and vibrations on a cellular level as I drifted off into a peaceful, quiet, and deep meditative state. The first image that came to mind, then body, was that familiar and wonderful childhood memory: playing my guitar. I pictured myself at nine years old, holding the cherished wooden instrument against my tiny chest. The magical, soothing resonance comforted my brain and body, as fingers strummed across the strings.

During the bowl session, peace enveloped me, and I attained one of the most relaxing meditative states. As a nurse and researcher, I thought, "What is my heart rate and blood pressure now, compared to when I arrived? Would it be lower and consistent with this current blissful state of mind and body?" And there it was. Brenda's words echoed in my mind: *Jayan, follow your bliss.*

Learning there was a paucity of empirical qualitative or quantitative research studies examining HSB effects, I knew what I would be researching for the next three to five years. As quick and powerful as a lightning bolt strike, the HSB experience created the charge needed to complete phase two of my doctoral work. Using prior research skills from graduate studies at Boston College, along with having access to great thinkers on my mentor team, I set out to prove or disprove HSB effects on the central nervous system. My doctoral research study examined blood pressure, heart rate and emotional responses to HSB exposure, using a traditional Western approach to study this Eastern complementary alternative method (CAM).

ACKNOWLEDGMENTS

My Village

Completion of my doctoral work was made possible with guidance and support from many individuals. I thank my primary mentor, Dr. Thomas Page, for his enthusiasm, belief, ongoing advice and assistance throughout the research phase. I am grateful to the study participants for generously volunteering their time, and to my former husband Paul R. Conlin M.D., endocrinologist and professor of medicine at Harvard Medical School, who offered valuable knowledge and support. Gratitude is extended to my daughter Elizabeth, mother Lorette, brother Joe, sister Patty, and friends Ruthie Crow, Lindsay Waller, Wendy Delaney, Betsey Beaven, Joyce Hashem, Linda Desjardins, Gina Bonanno, Helen Williams, Kathy Larocque, Donna Martin, and Diane Lovallo who helped me realize in various ways during that time that "I can do anything I set my mind to."

I acknowledge and honor past and present Trauma Intervention Program of Merrimack Valley (TIP) volunteers and board members, public service personnel, community supporters, fellow nurses, survivors, and private practice patients, who have been my greatest teachers. Together, for the past twenty-two years, we have learned how to survive, healing our trauma, grief, and losses side by side in the trenches of trial and tribulation. I remain grateful for the many blessings God continues to bestow upon me in my personal, professional, and spiritual life. And with this book, it is possible for me to share knowledge and wisdom gained thus far from my own healing journey. To Brenda, whose spirit lives on:

Believe. How beautiful a day can be
when friendship touches it.

Please note: the Landry Method is not to be used as a substitute for proper medical care. If you have high blood pressure, please consult with your physician.

Cover photo provided by my gifted nephew Chris Gionet, a talented photographer and musician who has volunteered countless hours of technical support over the years.

INTRODUCTION

By the time I was a nine-year-old girl, I learned how to activate the healing power within me. My parents divorced when I was seven, back in the sixties. I did not know anyone who was dealing with the painful fallout from this particularly challenging life circumstance. Family counseling and private therapy were not the norm in our little New England town. In general, the approach to raising *kids* was captured in the belief that "children are to be seen and not heard." This philosophy was often embraced by our stepfather, who emulated *All in the Family's*, Archie Bunker.

So from an early age, my little spirit wanted to be heard, and that included my voice. I didn't know it then, but what I needed was a way to cope with the stressors imposed on my young life-not necessarily *caused* by the divorce but rather how the adults *managed* in the aftermath from their own lack of ability and resources.

The following Christmas, I unwrapped a life-changing gift, my first guitar. When my small fingers strummed across the six nylon strings, I felt the vibrations being released and involuntarily slipped into a relaxed, trancelike state. In this new place, I felt calm and peaceful. No matter how stressful my life had become, with each pluck and stroke, I could access this unique, soothing vibration. When adding my voice to the guitar strum, the resonance offered a pleasing combination, echoing deep in my chest. It was empowering to be the creator of this reverberation, transporting me to a *tranquil place* as my body came into contact with the back of the rosewood.

Scarlett Parent was born outside Paris, France, to a family of talented performers. I had the good fortune when, at the age of two, she moved to the United States and lived in the house next to mine. Blessings continued when she became my friend and guitar teacher. Being a few years older, Scarlett shared what she learned during her weekly lessons. While we practiced the challenging task of simultaneously strumming and singing together, we transformed ourselves as we tuned and turned inward to this magical place. Here, no worldly problems existed. Our big decisions included who would sing harmony and what fret would best represent our vocal ranges while we learned new songs, one chord at a time. Hours flew by like minutes. Either dinnertime or the onset of street lights signaled us to stop. Like an itch that needed to be scratched, playing the guitar and singing was meeting more needs than I could have understood. The time I spent making music with Scarlett became the most important part of my week. I didn't know it then, but this would become one of my most essential tools for coping and healing both adolescent and adult challenges.

On a summer day, when I was 12 and Scarlett 14, we were performing on my front porch (our stage) across from the local cemetery on Main Street. We enthusiastically sang and strummed without fear of judgment, for the residents of the quiet cemetery audience never booed us. Larry Coleman, a classmate of Scarlett's, walked by. He must have been drawn in by our acoustic aptitude and brilliance, for he walked to the front steps and asked to join us. Proudly announcing he was a drummer, we agreed to expand our porch band. Larry went home and returned swiftly, carrying a crumbled paper bag. Kneeling on the porch, he quietly unpacked his gear: three shoeboxes and a set of sticks. He jumped right in as we played John Denver's "Take Me Home, Country Roads." With each beat of Larry's drum boxes, I felt the *thud* inside my chest. His special brand of percussion added a unique and distinctively deeper resonance and synchronicity to the music our new group was creating. Larry's contribution, like any great drummer or bass player, added the *soul* to our songs, enriching the ensemble as the three of us played as one during that summer.

Through Facebook I was pleased to learn that music remains an important part of their adult lives as well. With decades behind our childhood connection, Scarlett and I met in the past year to play again and sing our favorites for her older sister Nadege (another supportive force in my young life). We sang for Nadege as she courageously faced a terminal illness that sadly could not be overcome. She died within that year. Larry is a successful pilot and coincidentally lives in the town next to mine with his family. He continues to possess a deep appreciation for all kinds of music, especially jazz and the sounds of a saxophone.

After high school, I followed in my older sister Nancy's footsteps and became a registered nurse. That wise career choice opened many doors; nurse practitioner in medical nursing, years of hospital-based practice, clinical nurse specialist in mental health nursing, and private practice. Being drawn toward victims of emotional trauma, I was privileged to co-found and direct our non-profit Trauma Intervention Program of Merrimack Valley, Inc. (TIP) since 1993. Wayne Fortin founded the first TIP program in San Diego, CA in 1985.

For the past two decades, it has been inspiring and motivating to be a part of the healing power provided by our well-trained TIP volunteers. Acting as citizens helping citizens, they arrive on scene to offer a special brand of support at one of the worst times in someone's life. The letters of gratitude and praise we receive include words such as, "angel, miracle, life-changing" to describe the TIP volunteer's presence.

Having benefitted from over three decades of prior nursing, trauma intervention and personal healing experiences, while conducting research for my doctorate in counseling psychology, my curiosity was peaked regarding the effects of sound resonance and coping.

Could the sound and tone of guitar playing through the years, have had a positive effect on my personal physiology?

Could those childhood guitar and vocal reverberations have augmented my physical and mental health?

Could a Himalayan singing bowl offer the same healing effects?

This book will attempt to offer answers to those questions.

In Section 1, I will share a number of mental health concepts referred to as "pearls of wisdom." They include helpful strategies gained through prior nursing, trauma intervention, and private practice experiences. I chose the pearl analogy, for natural ones are created when certain shellfish, exposed to an irritant, release fluid, creating the lustrous beauty and value of the gem. Similarly, we have the ability to create personal treasures as we heal our injured lives.

Section 2 will include my HSB research dissertation. The technique created and implemented resulted in lowering blood pressure, heart rate, and negative affect states among the study participants. Empirical data analysis and results including all detailed charts and graphs are included.

Section 3 will tie it all together as you learn the Landry Method with an easy step-by-step approach. This method of playing the HSB followed by listening to the directed relaxation was created as a stress management tool and derived from research results shared in Section 2.

For those in my study, when the Himalayan singing bowl response was initiated, blood pressure and negative affect states decreased. Logically, what follows is the potential for greater health and well-being. I offer the Landry Method as a relaxation tool for your emotional first aid toolbox. My overall goal, for you as my reader, is to offer hope through healing along with new skills to aid in stress reduction, anger and blood pressure management. By the time you are finished reading this book, maybe you will consider adding my pearls and HSB therapy to your self-care and wellness routine.

My success will be measured by my ability to affect one person's life in a positive way. The following quote is another favorite that represents the fruits of the Spirit at work in me.

> To laugh often and much; To win the respect of intelligent people and the affection of children; To earn the appreciation of honest critics and endure the betrayal of false friends; To appreciate beauty, to find the best in others; To leave the world a bit better, whether by a healthy child, a garden patch, or a redeemed social condition; To know even one life has breathed easier because you have lived. This is to have succeeded.[3]
>
> —Bessie Anderson Stanley &
> Joseph Mitchell Chapple

SECTION 1

PEARLS OF WISDOM

PEARL NUMBER ONE

A FEW THOUGHTS ABOUT RESILIENCE

You may have heard it said, "When your time is up, it's up."

Conversely, if we are meant to be here on earth, we will be protected in ways that make it so. Throughout the years, while healing personal and others' trauma, I have learned to *lean into* faith while appreciating how fragile and resilient we are as a species. No matter what pain is suffered at the hands of another or through circumstances beyond our control, we have the marvelous ability to heal. In most situations we *can* survive the most unimaginable losses, and many of us will even learn to thrive as life is embraced once again.

On May 26, 1999, I was conducting a Training Academy with new trainees for our Trauma Intervention Program of Merrimack Valley, Inc. (TIP). The topic was resilience. During a break, while scanning our local community newspaper, *Lawrence Eagle-Tribune*, I came across an effective although somewhat dramatic article to help make a point to my prospective volunteers. The eye-catching headline was "Baby Survives Birth in Train Toilet, Fall on Tracks."

A newborn boy survived a fall through the
toilet of a Chinese express train, escaping with

only cuts and bruises after tumbling onto the rails, state media reported.

The boy's mother, Yang Zhu, was nine months pregnant and going home by train on May 4 when she began to suffer stomach pains, the Xinhua News Agency said in a report late Sunday.

Her husband took her to the washroom where, "to her great surprise," she gave birth to her first child into the toilet "as soon as she squatted down," Xinhua said.

"The panic-stricken and screaming Yang ripped off the umbilical cord with her hands, and the baby immediately slipped down through the toilet and fell onto the rails," the agency said.

Three security guards patrolling outside the southeastern city of Guangzhou spotted the baby, covered in blood and lying in the middle of the tracks, Xinhua said. But before they could reach him, another train sped by right over the baby.

The guards took the 5-pound, 15-ounce baby to a hospital, where he only had slight bruises and a small cut to the head that required three stitches.[4]

After reading the story, the trainees' incredulous expression matched my own when I initially read it. Two decades later, the story continues to make the point about resiliency in our academy.

Personally and professionally, in the midst of great grief and pain, one of the most useful strategies I can offer is the ability to envision the resiliency and adaptability of those I am helping. When working with clients, neighbors, friends, or loved ones who are dealing with an acute crisis, the helper bears witness to the individual's *ground zero*. The struggle may involve the death of a loved one due to heart attack, stroke, overdose, suicide, motor vehicle accident, cancer, or chronic illness, or total loss due to a devastating house fire or domestic crisis. In my private practice setting, clients will also present with symptoms of anxiety or depression due to long-standing mental health or medical conditions. Situational crises such as a divorce, relationship changes, financial stressors, terminal diagnoses, addictions, job termination, and concerns regarding children are all powerful motivators for seeking help. While bearing witness and empathizing with clients, helpers may experience a dose of the pain as well (vicarious traumatization). This happens when we either drop down into the painful grief pit with them or offer a lifeline to help them climb out.

Conceptualizing resilience, even in the worst circumstances, aids in emotionally protecting both the helper and the person in need. Imagining my clients in a future state of being healed and capable of coping in healthy ways gives me the strength to hold their intense emotional affect in the crisis moment. Being fully present and grounded in *my* senses while gazing into the eyes of a parent who just lost a child, or a child who just buried a parent, I envision resilience and visualize he or she coming out the other side of the tunnel toward greater well-being. With appropriate support and guidance, most clients will find peace and, for many, joy in their lives as they *grow* forward through the dark days of pain, grief, and loss. Many will mend far past surviving and begin to thrive in their future lives. And for those victim advocates who come to offer help, the most effective will possess a passion for healing others, which is often rooted in agonizing personal circumstances.

I have no illusions. When we lose a loved one, life is never the same. The grievers have the monumental task of learning how to live without their beloved for the remainder of their days. Most people are capable, some more than others. How is that possible? I believe in a number of likely variables that help determine the outcome when *healing emotional trauma*. The individual has the:

- innate desire for change
- inner strength that comes from past challenge management
- supportive resources (access to knowledge and helpful people)
- attitude of tenacity and persistence
- faith in a higher power
- hope that goodness will prevail
- willingness to evaluate and revise—shifting from Plan A to Plan B as needed (resiliency and flexibility)
- sense of humor about self, others, and circumstances
- presence of positive role models (good therapists are in this category)
- absence of addictions to numb and/or avoid pain
- ability to accept and manage mental and/or physical limitations
- desire for a hopeful future
- ability to seek knowledge about wellness attainment
- ability to find purpose or meaning in the loss (this may take decades)
- option to choose love over anger or bitterness
- ability to empathize by seeing the situation from another person's perspective
- attitude of positivity

- ability to accept reality as it is, not as you would like it to be
- ability to forgive

Forgiveness

African Grief Story: "The Interpreter"

It is said that in Matobo, Africa, everyone who loses somebody wants revenge on someone else, even God if no one else is available. In this particular African tribe, members believe the only way to end grief is to save the life of another. The "drowning mantra" ritual occurs when someone is murdered. A year of mourning ends and is followed by an all-night party/ ritual beside a river. At dawn, the killer is put into a boat, taken out on the water, bound, and dropped in. The grieving family must make a choice: either let the killer drown, or they must swim out to save him.

They believe that if the grieving family lets the killer drown, they will have justice, but will spend the rest of their lives in mourning. If they choose to save him, while admitting life isn't always fair, that very act can take away their sorrow.

Years of private practice and intermittent personal strife have taught me that *vengeance is a lazy form of grief.* I heard it said that holding onto resentment, anger or a grudge is like setting yourself on fire and hoping the other person dies from the fumes. Those who harbor years of bitterness and resentment, hanging onto rage as a life preserver, have skipped over some important grief work steps. It is called work for a reason. Going through the tunnel is difficult, and many opt out thinking that by going around it instead, they will avoid pain. But that won't get you where you need to go, for pain in some form is inevitable if we have loved. One may temporarily sidestep grief tasks by using overwork, isolation, addictive behaviors or substances to numb out. Without the luxury of time and effort required to grieve or the use of skillful helpers to aid in the healing process, grief usually comes out sideways months or years later. Sideway symptoms often manifest as anxiety, depressive disorders, or other medical and mental health illnesses. If bitterness and revenge fantasies accompany the grief process, it is likely that some kind of action requiring "letting go," such as that illustrated in the African drowning ritual, may lead one out of being stuck while progressing on the path to full healing.

Much of the resilience I appreciate as an adult grew from childhood challenges where I learned to cope by taking responsibility for myself coupled with some kind of action. My parents' divorce when I was seven, exposure to our alcoholic step-father, a sexual assault at seventeen (within weeks of my father dying of a heart attack at the age of fifty) and at twenty, the death of my first boyfriend. In each of these situations, the lack of professional support during that time in my life made it more difficult to manage. I am certain that some of my pain and suffering would have been mitigated if I had greater access to some of the successful healing variables listed earlier.

However, what I did possess was the ability to put my God faith into action along with an attitude of persistence and tenacity. I became stronger, like the fibrous tissue that grows over a fresh wound. The action steps I chose to take along the way led me to become a grateful survivor and fierce victim advocate.

As an adult, I had a miracle of my own, only God could have orchestrated. The miracle changed my life by offering me a personal opportunity to forgive. There was an unusual set of circumstances on a TIP call I was on, which lead to the healing of a personal trauma that had happened decades earlier. Let's start with the trauma.

At seventeen, I was sexually assaulted, by my supervisor from my after school job. The traumatic, unexpected, confusing encounter was serious enough to result in surgery and a three-day hospital stay. Sadly, no TIP volunteers or counselors of any kind were available to help me understand, process and heal in the immediate aftermath. Numbed out and bathed in shock, my second injury came from the shame I felt when the surgeon (who never asked what happened), looked down at me lying on the gurney in the Emergency Room and stated for all within earshot: "looks like you had one heck of a time for yourself last night young lady." Post-operative, groggy from anesthesia and pain medication, I blamed the incident on a gymnastic injury and was relieved when those closest to me believed my story. I didn't share the truth with anyone. I used denial, buried the pain and confusion deep inside, and went into nursing school in my effort to learn how to heal myself, and the world. Even though I never spoke of the incident again, I would later learn that my psyche and body didn't forget one detail of that memorable night. My body was keeping the score and on a cellular level, it was all being stored away and manifesting in ways I am still learning about to this day, surprisingly, many are positive. I will explain that part later.

At the time, I was in my late thirties, and on call for the Trauma Intervention Program. I volunteered to pick up a last-minute shift for another team member on a Sunday night. Five minutes before my shift was to end, at the request of the local police, I responded to a home in my town. The call was typical. Assistance was required to comfort and support an elderly woman in crisis (we'll call her Bessy). Her sister died at the dinner table. The Emergency Medical Technician (EMT) at the scene introduced me to Bessy, who was quite emotional and bedridden.

Her needs became my priority as she asked me to notify her sister's son of the death and request that he come to her right away. Having no phone of her own, I offered mine and dialed her nephew. As I dialed, Bessy told me her nephew's name, where he lived and worked. Immediately realizing the nephew was my perpetrator from over twenty years ago, my mouth went dry. Coincidence?

Staying professional in the helper role, I handed Bessy my phone and remained at her bedside as she informed him that his mother died while eating dinner. Hearing his pained voice and sobs projecting from my phone speaker, I connected with the pain *I* had experienced when I heard of my father's sudden death at seventeen. Filled with compassion, I felt connected— almost united—with this man who had harmed me decades earlier.

The call ended, and Bessy's nephew was on his way. In an hour, he would be standing in my spot. Bessy proceeded to share that my perpetrator grew up in an abusive, alcoholic home. She was proud of him, for he married, had children, and was working hard to break the cycle of abuse. Cerebrally, I took in her words, and spiritually I felt God's presence with me this second time I had contact with my abuser. But on this occasion, I would be safe from his harm, while being offered a miracle of my own I had yet to figure out.

I stayed exactly forty-five minutes before I left Bessy with support materials and office follow-up numbers. I broke my own rule of waiting for a replacement to arrive and departed. Bewildered, with heart pounding, I exited the house with palms open to the sky and spoke out loud to my God, "What is the meaning of this extraordinary circumstance? How could this TIP call have been a coincidence? I wasn't scheduled to be on duty today."

That evening, the blessings began to wash over me in the safety of my home as my brain thawed out of its frozen, protective shock state. Over twenty years of reading, writing, and trying to process and heal, and now I had been divinely led to a bedside seat the moment my perpetrator heard of his mother's death—hearing his sobs firsthand from *my* cell phone. What message was God compelling me to hear?

Like most survivors in the aftermath of something really big happening, I was driven to share my experience. When a trusted and loving "other" bears witness to our story, we are comforted and begin the work of finding meaning. I called my brother Joe (agnostic at the time) to describe the events of this unusual Sunday evening. He was loving and supportive while listening intently. He could not help but have his own spiritual curiosity peaked as I drew the line from my childhood assault experience to the evening events bridging the gap of over twenty years.

Soul deep, I knew only God could have blessed me with that personal Sunday night experience. I had been angry long enough about what was taken from me that evening many years ago. Flooded with intense emotions that now felt nothing like pain or anger, strangely, I *connected* with my perpetrator, who also grew up in a stressful household fueled by alcohol addiction. My tender heart cracked open. Empathy and compassion for *him* began to flow.

God offered the gift of hearing my perpetrator's cries and allowed me to peek into the window of his abusive childhood home. And in the soil under the windowsill's ledge, my empathy for him planted the seeds of compassion and forgiveness that would lead to my next place of personal healing.

Through my professional experiences, I have adopted the philosophy that we are all born innocent— then life events happen, changing who we are and the choices we make. I discovered that boys who suffer child abuse without proper treatment often act aggressively toward others as adults, and girls who suffer abuse are often victims themselves. Hurt people often hurt other people. Who do I hurt if I carry around a life-sucking grudge, draining precious energy, and all the while feeling sorry for myself? Me.

It took a few more years, but eventually with the help of great friends, family, spiritual and secular counselors, I dropped my hidden desire for revenge and healed from my pain and trauma. I was able to let it go—for me. With the help of God, I swam into the water and rescued the bound man, while He moved me to total forgiveness without my perpetrator knowing any of it. Whenever someone offers forgiveness a prisoner is set free, and that prisoner is the one doing the forgiving. I was free.

God used all the pain to create the passion fueling my desire to spend most of my adult life as a victim advocate and healer. Those facing trauma in our community do not have to do it alone. In the months and years that followed that very special TIP call, He continues to give me numerous opportunities to work with people hurt by similar circumstances offering counsel from a personal perspective.

The power of forgiveness and finding meaning in loss healed my soul as I transitioned from victim to survivor.

Finding Meaning in Loss

The psychiatrist Viktor Frankl was imprisoned in a Nazi concentration camp during the Second World War. During his imprisonment, he tried to understand why some inmates were able to survive the unbelievably demeaning and degrading experience, without losing their humanity, while others crumbled. He concluded that those who survived emotionally were able to find some kind of meaning in this most **un**understandable of circumstances. For some, meaning came in the form of a new conviction or promise they made to themselves upon release. Maybe they would devote their lives to sharing their camp experiences. Others survived by determining to help those during encampment, even as they were personally suffering so deeply. Once we have found meaning in the most trying events that may happen to us, we can face them with the energy of a survivor. Out of his observations, Frankl wrote the book *Man's Search for Meaning*,[5] which explores this topic with more depth.

With society's drive-through mentality for everything from food to dry cleaning, patience is an important part of the recovery process. When getting from where we are to where we want to be, we learn to be patient with this "in-between" place. Decisions and actions you make while enduring the "in-between" will have an impact on the overall quality of your life. Seeking healthy self-care is a good option, for waiting is a necessary part of movement.

Healing childhood grief and trauma is a lifelong journey marked by exacerbations and remissions, but also sprinkled with encouragement, hope, and relief. Lessons learned are byproducts of these experiences. Through enduring and healing the pain from suffering, we develop that unique capacity to successfully relate to others in crisis. This gift of wisdom transforms into clarity of awareness, and empathy often emerges. I continually marvel at how God uses the enlightened ones to effectively deliver the exact words and actions needed at just the right time and in the right way, to help heal another's anguish.

Personal change that emerges with effective trauma management is often referred to as post-traumatic growth (PTG). For many survivors, PTG will manifest in a life filled with greater strength and more meaning, while dispelling the notion that trauma leads to dysfunction. This is also true with childhood challenges, which often become the building blocks for a better view. In some cases, they are the stepping-stones to a healthier place throughout adulthood.

With the maturity and wisdom gained through pain, we all have a second chance to create a new life by putting these healing principles into action. As Helen Reddy sang, it is truly "wisdom born of pain" that we eventually come to appreciate and honor as the decades swiftly pass by. All along the way, we pay the emotional, physical, or mental health price for that pain. But then comes the gain with the inner knowledge that you *can* do anything through your newfound strength and sense of invincibility.

I celebrate each personal crisis, for they have laid the groundwork to continue finding relevant meaning and purpose in my life. Learning to cope and manage painful experiences has equipped me with the ability to guide and facilitate in the healing of others. Most of all, I am grateful for and proud of the wisdom gained from every single moment spent here on this earth— in joy and in pain.

PEARL NUMBER TWO

HOW DO YOU DEFINE STRESS?

Most of us live in a world filled with daily stressors while being challenged to manage multiple demands on our time and energy. Part of being human includes being subjected to stressful and possibly traumatic events. A key concept to keep in mind is that our *perception* of the event will play a large role in how we manage. One may view a particular state of affairs as stressful and traumatic, and another will see the same situation or set of circumstances as an opportunity for change and growth. This depends on a number of internal and external variables. Internal variables may include the individual's prior knowledge, experience, resilience, and coping abilities. External variables include the duration and timing of the event, prior life stressors, and related circumstances, along with the nature and depth of the relationship between the person and the loved one involved.

What we do know in the field of trauma intervention is that traumatic events are a great equalizer. None of us has immunity, and trauma does not discriminate based on socioeconomic, demographic, or geographic factors. When considering our ability to cope, keep in mind that our well-being is not so much determined by the events in our lives but rather how we *view* and *cope* with these events. For the purpose of our discussion, stress can be understood as your response to an upsetting or traumatic situation. John Milton makes the point another way: he sees the mind is its own place, and it can make a heaven of hell and a hell of heaven.[6] How you view and manage the situation, is key and also within your power to control.

In *The How of Happiness*, Sonja Lyubomirsky argues that one's happiness is fifty percent determined by genetics (happiness set point); forty percent by habits, behaviors, and thought patterns; and only ten percent by our life circumstances (how much money we have, where we live, who we live with, life events connected with our perception of happiness).[7] This is good news, for while we may not have much control over what the universe serves up for us—we do have some control over genetic and attitude management, which account for 90 percent of how happy we are.

Therapy and medication can help address issues genetically or attitudinally, inherited or adopted, such as anxiety, depression, addictions and mental health challenges, thought patterns, and coping strategies. Therefore, our energy is best spent on learning how to effectively view and manage the events in our lives, versus ruminating and feeling sorry for ourselves due to the situations we find ourselves in.

Examples of Stressful/Traumatic Events

Any of these situations can cause stress and/or trauma in your life: death of a loved one, home invasion, separation, divorce, poor relationship quality, loss of a job, conflict with boss or coworker, birth of a child, infidelity, coping with a beloved's mental illness, military trauma, managing your or a loved one's addiction, marital/relationship conflict among family or friends, grief over any loss, infertility, pet death, chronic pain, long-term illness management, financial strain, breakup with partner, jail term, house fire, suicide or homicide death of a loved one, retirement, aging parents with supervision needs, only child leaving home, working full-time while taking courses to further your career, rape, physical assault, home and/ or job relocation, sexual identity/orientation issues, or hearing news you or a loved one has a terminal diagnosis.

This list, while not complete, offers a glimpse of various challenges dealt daily to the human race. Remember, we are not so much determined by the actual situations but rather how we view them and what we do to cope. Traumatic events often occur without warning, but we have some control over how we manage the situation, and that directly impacts our physical and mental well-being.

Two men looked out from prison bars; one
saw the mud, the other saw the stars.
—Dale Carnegie [8]

They are both in the same prison cell, but one looks up and takes comfort and delights in the magnificence of the stars (grateful survivor), and the other chooses to look down and focus on the miserable mud (ungrateful victim). Which one are you? How hardy are you? If you are willing to take action, you can evolve from an ungrateful victim to a grateful survivor. We will continue to explore the survivor and victim concepts throughout the first section of this book.

PEARL NUMBER THREE

HOW HARDY ARE YOU?

Hardiness—the ability to endure difficult conditions

Dr. Salvatore Maddi (1999)[9,10] characterized hardiness as a combination of three attitudes: challenge, control, and commitment. These three C's give us the courage and ability to turn stressful or traumatic events from the potential disasters they are into opportunities for personal growth. Using Dr. Maddi's three C's of hardiness, I've designed this short quiz to see how hardy you are. Answer the following questions as they relate to the trauma examples offered in the last section, or in relation to your current personal struggle.

Dr. Landry's Hardiness Quiz

Once the initial shock has abated, when faced with a traumatic event:

1. Do you see it as a *challenge* versus a *threat* to your well-being or survival?
2. Do you begin to look for solutions?
3. Do you reach out to others who can help you gather resources to cope?

4. Do you have an optimistic and hopeful attitude about the event?

5. Do you feel you are in control of your own attitude about your destiny?

6. Are you committed to surviving this event by making efforts to care for yourself (make healthy nutrition choices, get seven to eight hours of sleep a night, exercise at least twenty minutes three to four times a week, and practice deep-breathing exercises, meditation, or relaxation techniques)?

7. Do you stick with positive ways of coping listed in question 6, or do you turn to drugs, alcohol, sex, food, work, and/or overspending to manage painful or anxious thoughts and feelings?

If you did not answer yes to all seven questions, the good news is you now have a starting place toward improved wellness.

Questions one through three address your ability to view the event as a challenge that must be overcome versus a potential disaster that will "take you down." Get busy looking for solutions, and mobilize people, places, and things to help you manage. Call a safe and knowledgeable contact person, and utilize the Internet to locate therapists, volunteers, or support/church groups who can offer assistance.

What makes someone a *safe* contact person? When we are hurting, we are vulnerable and need to surround ourselves with safe people. My definition of a safe person is simple:

Safe contact person: After you have any contact (via phone, Internet, e-mail, in person) you feel better versus worse.

I appreciate and understand that using my definition of a safe person may eliminate a number of family members or friends you have reached out to in the past or may currently be in your life. While I'm not suggesting you remove people from your life (although that may be needed), I am suggesting when you are dealing with a life-changing *SEE* (significant emotional event), you may consider confiding your personal details with only those who make you feel better after having contact versus worse. It is not unusual to have a therapist as your safest person during a crisis. A therapist, as an objective outsider, can understand and support the sharing of highly personal feelings and details while keeping strict confidences. If you meet with a therapist three times and do not feel he or she is helpful, give up on the therapist not on therapy, and keep searching. It is a very personal relationship, and you must feel comfortable and safe. We come in all shapes and sizes, and finding the right match for both client and therapist is part of the process.

There are varying levels of intimate communication sharing. High-level sharing includes personal details about your situation and your feelings, and low-level consists of less intimate details, such as current events like the weather conditions. The latter conversation may be the kind you have with your hairdresser or acquaintances. This low-level sharing is best reserved for the emotionally *unsafe* family and friends while you are in crisis. Take a few moments now to make a list of your safe people, and let them be your starting place for reaching out.

Questions four and five address the aspect of control. We understand the universe and much of what happens in our life is not within our control, but we can control our response to it. Do you see yourself as the master of your own destiny, or are you a victim of your circumstances? Are you powerful or helpless? Choosing to be optimistic and hopeful during a difficult situation will allow the much-needed energy and power to move forward in healthy ways.

Questions six and seven address your level of commitment. In other words, when the going gets tough, the tough get going. How tough are you?

Do you rally? Or do you run away physically or mentally by escaping into the world of addictions, distractions, and other forms of self-harm and neglect? If there was ever a time for your strongest physical, mental, and spiritually sound self, it is during stressful and traumatic events. In the words of Marcus Aurelius, the joint sixteenth emperor of the Roman Empire:

> Our life is what our thoughts make it. If we think
> happy thoughts, we will be happy; if we think
> miserable thoughts, we will be miserable.[11]

The good news is we can control our thoughts and learn how to be more optimistic.

If Marcus's quote makes you think of Eleanor H. Porter's best-selling novel *Pollyanna*,[12] keep in mind that at the very least, positive thoughts will help us harness the energy we need to deal with our stressful event, and negative thoughts will take our precious energy away. Survivors rise and rally; victims are martyrs, who feel pity for themselves, lie down, and give up. Which one are you? Which one do you want to be?

For spiritual support, when positive thinking needs reinforcement, my favorite Bible verse keeps me centered and on track:

> Finally, brothers and sisters, whatever is noble, whatever
> is right, whatever is pure, whatever is lovely, whatever
> is admirable—if anything is excellent or praiseworthy—
> think about such things. Whatever you have learned or
> received or heard from me, or seen in me-put it into
> practice. And the God of peace will be with you.
> —Philippians 4:8-9 New International Version[13]

PEARL NUMBER FOUR

VICTIM OR SURVIVOR?

In an effort to make the point of victim versus survivor with clients, I use my sailboat analogy. Pretend you are alone on a sailboat enjoying a warm, sun-filled day off the coast of Cape Cod, Massachusetts. You've been sailing for hours and have consumed your nutritional snacks and fresh water supply. You are getting hot, hungry, and thirsty. In the distance, you spot a restaurant on the harbor shoreline filled with lively patrons. This oasis is quite far away, and the wind has ceased to blow. Your sails are still; now you have choices to make regarding how to manage your new, uncomfortable reality.

Choice One: Victim

Your brain begins to release a series of negative thoughts that you instantly accept. It may sound like this: "I *should* have packed more water and food (should statements imply judgment). My wife/husband should have packed more water and food (blaming others). I *feel* stupid, so I *am* stupid (emotional reasoning). I was *dumb* to pick this day to sail (labeling). I *always pick the worst* days to sail (overgeneralization). If there's going to be a no-wind day, it will be the day I pick to go sailing (all or nothing thinking, self-pity). Maybe I'm being punished (filtering). This is a disaster (catastrophizing, discounting the positives). I am going to dehydrate out here, and no one will find me (negatively predicting the future, jumping to conclusions). No one cares anyway (jumping to conclusions)."

The words above in parentheses are a few of the main cognitive distortions pioneered by the psychiatrist Aaron Beck in the 1960s.[14] He found that depressed patients experienced this kind of rapid, negative thought stream he called automatic thoughts. These automatic thoughts fell into three categories. As in my illustration above, patients had negative thoughts about—

1) themselves
2) the world
3) the future

Dr. Beck was able to help his patients notice and evaluate these automatic thoughts. Patients were then taught to think more realistically, talk back to the thoughts (which helped them feel better emotionally), and have a higher level of functioning. Patients who changed their underlying beliefs about themselves, their world, and other people had long-lasting benefits. Dr. Beck called this approach cognitive behavior therapy (what the mind thinks affects our behavior). So, if we can change our thoughts, we can change our behavior. In a moment I will discuss how our automatic neurochemistry soup adds to the impact of this cognitive distortion problem. For a good practical understanding of cognitive distortions and ways to manage them, I highly recommend *Feeling Good* by Dr. David Burns (1999).[15]

Dr. Daniel Amen's *Change Your Brain, Change Your Life* (1998) offers us another way to understand this cognitive distortion concept, using the acronym ANTS, which stands for automatic negative thoughts.[16] When the first *ant* arrives at our picnic, if we do not remove it immediately, soon many of its friends will join in to ruin our fun. Numerous negative thoughts in our mind cause aggravation and possibly ruin our good time or peace of mind like any real ants at our picnic. Therefore, it is best to stop the first automatic negative thought in its tracks, for what we allow our mind to focus on gets stronger and larger. I teach my clients to become familiar with the cognitive distortions from my examples above, recognize them swiftly, stop feeding them attention, and immediately replace with a healthy, positive thought or activity. What we draw our attention to gets larger—the good or the bad—and the choice is up to you. This process may need to be repeated a hundred times a day depending on how entrenched this line of thinking has been for you. But over time you will create a healthier brain track by setting your new default to positive thoughts and actions. Valuable and productive energy naturally flows from there.

Let's go back to our boat analogy and the negative victim statements. If you think; "I *should* have done this or that; I am stupid, dumb, and continue to make mistakes; this always happens to me; and I know this is a disaster and will turn out badly," you are now persecuting yourself and entering into the self-pity zone, which never ends well.

Most problems have solutions so consider spending time and energy on the solution, not the problem. Re-direct any self-pity for it is wasted energy. I appreciate Maya Angelou's thoughts on self-pity. In its early stage, it is "snug as a feather mattress," but when it hardens, it becomes uncomfortable.[17] I am challenging you to avoid spending excessive time in your feather mattress. Feel your pain, but if you get stuck in self-pity, seek the wisdom of others to help you know when it's time to use your featherbed as a springboard to propel you out, and back into taking control of your life.

Anxiety and/or panic often follow self-pity. Negative changes automatically occur within your body. From that faulty thought place *you* created in your brain using cognitive distortions, you respond accordingly to ensure survival. You flood your bloodstream and organs with stress chemicals, such as cortisol and norepinephrine, which are designed to help you get through a *true* crisis. These potent neurochemicals arise from the primitive, survival portions in our brain. This response is required when faced with life-threatening situations, calling for action in the emergency. However, when we manifest this state by chronically imagining the "what if" in our mind, it leads to disease. There is a better way, and I propose choice two.

Choice Two: Survivor

This second choice comes from being a survivor of the no wind situation. The survivor sounds more like this: "Wow, this is a challenge. I am hungry and thirsty, and there is no wind. But I am committed to getting to that restaurant. As master of my own destiny, I cannot wait for someone or something external (like the wind or another person) to solve this situational crisis for me. I've been in other jams before and always figured out how to get home. What are my options in the absence of wind or a rescuer?"

You garner what little energy you have left and begin a series of deep breathing exercises, the most important first-line coping strategy. This helps turn off the stress chemical faucet and allows you to focus on finding a solution. More clarity occurs as you imagine yourself in a calm, peaceful location. You may turn to your Higher Power in the form of prayer or meditation. As the oxygen from your deep breaths enhance calmness, you have access to your prefrontal cortex (the section of brain inside your forehead—your thinking brain), which helps with problem solving. With your prefrontal brain online and fully functioning, your neurochemicals under management, you now have a much greater ability to solve your dilemma. You are able to see the emergency oars stored beneath your seat (which you overlooked before when your thinking brain was off-line), and you begin the arduous but effective process of rowing yourself closer to the restaurant. As you rely on personal strength, you feel more empowered. You are patient, realistic and accepting the reality that it may take all day to reach your destination for food and water, but that is fine. Now, you are grateful there is no wind to push you back as you advance one meter at a time.

You are embracing the experience. Your self-induced state of encouragement generates additional strength. With each stroke, you build confidence in your own efficacy, enriching personal competence. As your body rallies to this eustress (good stress) condition, extra blood is shunted to your powerful heart, along with arm and leg muscles, which propel you forward with greater force. Eventually, you successfully arrive at your destination, and the reward center in your brain releases one of your "feel good" chemicals called dopamine. This organic high moves you to feel deeply grateful for the challenging opportunity, enabling you to grow stronger and wiser (not to mention you will have a great story to tell).

Dopamine acts like a save button in the brain when we learn something new. The more dopamine released during an event, the better we remember it. This reward center not only helps us stay focused but also encourages us to repeat activities reinforced through positive outcomes, such as our example of paddling ourselves to the shoreline.

When we experience something new, in addition to dopamine, the brain releases endorphins, which offer us a feeling of being naturally *high*. The successful experience reinforces your belief in your own capabilities, as you avoided the numerous detrimental effects of an unnecessary negative stress response. You are a survivor, not a victim. You feel good mentally and physically, as you tapped into the miraculous power of your body's ability to help you cope. The choice of victim versus survivor is always yours to make in both the large and small circumstances of your everyday life.

PEARL NUMBER FIVE:

HOMEMADE STRESS CHEMICAL SOUP

Within the brain, the autonomic nervous system (ANS) is located in the medulla oblongata. The ANS is our major control system for critical bodily functions such as heart rate, breathing, digestion, and arousal. There are three main branches:

Branch one: Jacks us up (sympathetic)—fight or flight

Branch two: Calms us down (parasympathetic)—rest and digest

Branch three: Digestion (enteric)

All are needed for survival. For the following discussion, we will focus on branches one and two.

Branch One: Sympathetic

We are grateful for branch one in action when we need it. Proper functioning of our sympathetic branch is one of our body's primary ways of ensuring survival. If you were being chased by a large hungry beast, branch one would be activated.

Your brain and kidneys' adrenal glands automatically release the perfect stress-coping chemical soup mixture, into your bloodstream. These stress hormones, including adrenaline, cortisol, and norepinephrine, are potent and designed to help you survive an immediate threat by opening your pupils wider while sharpening your vision, which enhances clarity as you attempt to escape the beast. As your strength increases, additional blood is shunted to larger muscles. With an increased heart rate, oxygen-rich blood moves into vessels and veins needed to fight or run away. Natural opioids deaden any pain interfering with this survival response.

The term *hysterical strength* has been used to define the intensity of this phenomenon, which demonstrates the effects of the hormone adrenaline. Adrenaline can increase strength to incredible degrees for short periods of time when needed during a crisis. Writer Jeff Wise granted permission to use his story, published in the November 2010 issue of *Psychology Today*, to illustrate this point:

> I saw the crumpled frame of a bike under the car's bumper, and tangled within it a boy, trapped. That's when Boyle got out and started running. For an agonizing eternity the Camaro screeched on, dragging the mass under it. As it slowed to a stop he could hear the bicyclist pounding on the car with his free hand, screaming. Without hesitating Boyle bent down, grabbed the bottom of the chassis, and lifted with everything he had. Slowly, the car's frame rose a few inches. The bicyclist screamed for him to keep lifting. Boyle strained. "It's off

me!" the boy yelled. Someone pulled him free, and Boyle let the car back down.

Boyle accomplished an almost unthinkable feat of strength. The world record for dead-lifting a barbell is 1,003 pounds. A stock Camaro weighs 3,000 pounds. How does the body unleash these reserves? The answer might lie in another, related aspect of the fear response: it deadens pain. Among the chemicals that the brain releases when under acute stress are two kinds, endocannabinoids and opioids, both powerful analgesics. Their painkilling effects override the aching feeling we normally get when we try to lift heavy weights. Unfortunately, the effect is temporary. After Boyle went home, the painkilling properties wore off, and he realized that he'd clenched his jaw so hard while lifting that he'd shattered eight teeth.[18]

The human body is indeed remarkable and mysterious. We are designed to survive and heal. Once we understand how to harness our body's natural chemistry, we have this powerful tool to access and then use as needed.

PEARL NUMBER SIX

GETTING A GRIP ON
ANXIETY AND ANGER

Lifting a three-thousand-pound Camaro to save a person's life is a good example of sympathetic branch one (jacks you up) in action, with help from the potent self-made adrenaline leading the charge in that extreme circumstance. Let's look at a few less dramatic examples that help illustrate how we can benefit from an awareness of how stress chemical soup affects our everyday life.

As a nurse and therapist, I find it helpful to use rating scales with my clients to measure anything from happiness with a relationship partner to anxiety, depression, anger, guilt, etc. This is often done during our first intake assessment meeting, and we can use the chosen number as a frame of reference to monitor future progression. I simply ask my clients to rate their anxiety, anger, happiness etc. on a scale of zero (indicating least) to ten (indicating most). When clients pause to think about the number in their current distressing circumstance, it often solidifies the situation more clearly and concretely, offering us a starting place for therapy. Take a moment to look over this self-assessment anxiety rating scale.

Self-Assessment Anxiety Rating Scale

Anxiety rating scale

←Less Anxious   More Anxious →

0 ..... 1 ..... 2 ..... 3 ..... 4 ..... 5 ..... 6 ..... 7 ..... 8 ..... 9 10

(Zero indicates less anxious and ten most anxious.)

Now let's put the scale into practice.

Example One: Anxiety Awareness

As your workday ends, you are tired and hungry while standing in the market checkout line with dinner in your basket. You notice mild anxiety brewing as you glance at the time and note the bank is your next needed stop and will be closing in five minutes. Using the above anxiety rating scale from zero to ten, suppose you rate yourself a two. The first step in being able to successfully manage your anxiety starts right here at the awareness and self-assessment level.

Let's go deeper now. Are you able to notice where you feel this minor (two) annoyance in your body? Maybe you feel slightly worried emotionally as your shoulders or jaw get tighter. If you noticed this subtle shift in your physical body, how do you manage the sensations connected to this two on the scale? If you did notice, this is your opportunity to bring the two down to a one or even a zero. You can easily do this by distracting yourself with the entertaining or educational periodicals on the endcap. Maybe this distraction actually inspired you to try a new recipe you saw in a cooking magazine. Did you use this time to your advantage by responding productively to texts or e-mails on your mobile device? In an effort to calm yourself further, you have started to use a deep breathing exercise while imagining yourself in a more peaceful place, such as the ocean's edge or at the top of a mountain enjoying the view.

If you were successful with your breathing and imaging, most likely the tightness in your shoulders and jaw began to relax as your two moved closer to zero. This would be a good example of self-care and being able to *affect regulate*, a term often used by therapists to describe this intervention. In private practice, clients who are successful at accepting adverse situations, are more likely to affect regulate and accordingly, have a higher level of well-being and competence in the world. On the contrary, those who do not check themselves at the two, and feed the negative feelings and thoughts, tend to swiftly move up the right side of the scale. These clients are more likely to struggle with symptoms of depression, anxiety, and addictions as the neurochemical soup pattern becomes more entrenched.

Continuing with our grocery store example, let's add a stressor to the existing situation. Standing in the checkout line, with your anxiety at a low-level two, the man in front of you collapses and falls backward. On reflex, your arms reach out for him as you attempt to break his fall. You are unsuccessful as he and his grocery basket tumble to the floor. Although he is alert and appears uninjured, there is a commotion as the overhead microphone requests a manager to your checkout line. You are relieved the man is unharmed, but the grocery clerk suggests you remain in place to help explain what happened. Suddenly, your level two anxiety (which you didn't manage) shoots up toward an eight or nine, as you realize you will not be getting to the bank before closing time. Do you fight against this situational reality with your mind and body, or do you accept it and begin implementing ways to calm yourself?

You may consider making a list of healthy coping strategies that will help when you feel minor distress brewing. I've included my suggestions at the end of this chapter to help get you started on your own plan. Now let's use the same scale format to rate anger with our grocery store example. This will help illustrate another important aspect of self-care.

Self-Assessment Anger Rating Scale

Anger rating scale

←Less Angry   More Angry→

0 ..... 1 ..... 2 ..... 3 ..... 4 ..... 5 ..... 6 ..... 7 ..... 8 ..... 9 10

(Zero indicates not angry and ten most angry.)

Example Two: Anger Awareness

We will use the beginning of the same checkout line scenario but now consider your anger versus anxiety. It is the end of your workday. You are tired and hurrying to get through the market checkout before the bank closes. As you wait with your groceries, mild anger is brewing as you glance at your watch. Using the anger rating scale from zero to ten, you are at two. Are you able to recognize the two and notice where you feel this minor anger in your body? Maybe you feel slightly irritated emotionally and your shoulders or jaw are getting tighter. How do you manage this two? Do you distract yourself in entertaining or productive ways by thumbing through cooking, health, sports, or glamour magazines? Do you decide to check your e-mails from your mobile device? Do you begin to breathe deeply and imagine yourself in a peaceful place? Are you able to get that two to shift down toward a one or zero? Maybe you do nothing about the two in this current state of irritation.

Suddenly, another shopper abruptly cuts in line and stands directly in front of you, without awareness that you are there. What is your first response? What does your mind think; what does your body do? Is your fight-or-flight (sympathetic branch one) mechanism instantly activated, kicking your two rating to a nine or ten? Are you using colorful language silently or audibly to describe your current state of mind? Using our zero-to-ten scale, can you imagine your score in this situation?

Keep in mind, as you advance up the right side of the anger or anxiety rating scale, *you* are the person getting negatively affected and harmed. The individual doing the irritating behavior is either unaware or aware and does not care. Your body is the one suffering as it creates the chemical soup designed to save you during a *true* emergency (fight or flight). Over time these stress chemicals will wreak havoc with your mind, body, and spirit.

Instead of accepting the harsh reality that you will miss getting to the bank on time and immediately implementing healthy strategies to manage this truth, your negative thoughts persist and escalate your anxious and/or angry state. (Yes, the truth will set you free). In the anxiety or angry example states we discussed, and at times in your life when you realize your expectations for time management were changed without your permission, you have choices to make. If you do not intervene on your own behalf to calm yourself, most likely you will continue to escalate up these scales with the help of body chemistry. Stress chemicals cause our moods to rapidly shift from peaceful and calm to irritated, angry, or fearful. Fueled by adrenaline, they are designed to appropriately offer us the immediate physical and emotional energy surge needed in a true crisis. As the next chapter will teach, misuse of our stress chemical soup over time actually causes mind, body, and spirit harm to you and those around you.

PEARL NUMBER SEVEN

CHEMICAL SOUP
EFFECTS—HARMFUL

In the absence of true crisis, when we create and allow germination of negative thoughts, we unnecessarily risk activating sympathetic (branch one) activity. Like gasoline on a fire, in moments of anxiety or anger stemming from real or imagined stress, physical effects are accelerated and take place in our bodies. Sympathetic activation causes sweating, increased heart rate, and shallow breathing while inhaling from your chest versus abdomen. This breath pattern can lead to dizziness and severely affect your ability to think clearly. Your jaw, shoulders, and chest may feel tighter and, in extreme conditions, can lead to panic attacks. The brain's prefrontal cortex (responsible for judgment, good thinking, and decision making) gets turned off when the primitive limbic system is turned on. You have successfully created all this energy in your body to fight or flee, but often you are trapped in the checkout line, or inside your head as you lie in bed during the middle of the night thinking of daily troubles. Making matters worse, you don't have access to your brain's thinking section (prefrontal cortex), which would facilitate constructive problem solving. Some claim you have about thirty percent less intelligence when you are angry. In addition, what goes up with stress chemicals (heart rate, energy level, sharpened focus) will come down, for crisis states are time-limited. Exhaustion and, if repeated over time, chronic wear and tear follow, which adversely affects your health and those being exposed to your *dis*ease.

Consider these points:

> How important is it to get upset about life's minor annoyances?

> How many minutes/hours do I want to live without access to my thinking brain?

> Do I want to create constant wear and tear, causing harmful effects for me and my loved ones, due to my inability to affect regulate?

> How can I learn to resolve stressful situations swiftly, without causing harm to myself, and others?

> Do I want to exhaust normal chemical response on minor issues, leaving me at risk for greater illness and less reserve when something major comes along?

Have you ever been in a crisis situation and questioned why you did or didn't say or do something in the moment? Most of us will identify with the example that follows, which illustrates how the primitive brain shuts off the thinking brain during a crisis. It's comforting to know for most of us, when the crisis is past, the thinking brain returns. Understanding the normal stress response will help you process, while being patient with yourself as you form strategies to respond.

Example of Hit-and-Run Insult

One of those sneaky, unsafe people in your life—(a coworker)—makes a comment directed at you over morning coffee. Seemingly innocuous to others, the insult is a direct hit to your ego state. It comes in the form of a "veiled" compliment, but your limbic system is activated (your truth), and this skillful coworker is intentionally out to get a reaction from you. I call such people "energy vampires." They are unable to ascertain authentic happiness for themselves, so they are on the prowl to steal it from others who appear stronger. They have honed the art of skillfully using put-downs often in the form of sarcasm: "I'm only kidding; can't you take a joke?" Jokes are funny, but if you are not laughing, it's not a joke.

Sarcasm is a form of verbal aggression with the intent to inflict pain on another. Sarcastic comments represent poor communication skills not associated with honesty and often include passive-aggressive motives. Other times, the comment stems from sheer ignorance but usually comes in a sudden, unexpected drive-by, hit-and-run fashion. When the cheap shot is thrown your way, if your ego is involved, your limbic system is aroused, and chemical soup causes your physical symptoms to enable fight or flight. The prefrontal cortex—the rational-thinking and problem-solving portion of your brain—is turned off due to these chemical reactions. We are rendered temporarily speechless for a good reason. Our brain has left the building! But then, once calm, a few hours later (or at 1:00 A.M.) we think of the perfect comeback (prefrontal cortex back online). Don't be too hard on yourself, for during the moment of insult, the *thinking* part of your brain got turned off as you were emotionally triggered.

Now, having more clarity about the limbic system, can you imagine using this knowledge in other situations? How much rational problem solving occurs during a heated argument with your loved one when the limbic system is turned on and the prefrontal cortex is turned off? That would be a good time to take an adult time-out and go for a walk to cool off your limbic brain, while letting your partner know you will return. Then, with both brains fully present, you can reconnect and resume problem solving.

Turning Off the Limbic System

My favorite first-line intervention to cool off the limbic system during a crisis is the ujjayi breathing technique. I learned ujjayi years ago from Diana Kiesel at Yang's Fitness Center during a yoga class. This easy technique keeps our prefrontal cortex functioning and engaged while under pressure. A full explanation about how to do ujjayi breathing along with a number of other easy-to-learn, immediate stress intervention strategies will be described in further detail in the following chapter. Remember, it takes a lot less effort to go from two to zero than nine or ten to zero on our rating scales.

Trauma Drama

Some individuals have become addicted to the stimulating effects of sympathetic branch one and intentionally provoke people in situations to elicit the emotional charge or "fix" they are seeking. You may have heard of "trauma drama" or "drama queens." These people may also suffer from certain personality disorders such as borderline, histrionic, or dependent, which can include impulsivity and volatility. They are often highly emotional and or dependent on others, while seeking attention or approval from sources outside of themselves. Some causes include a genetic predisposition, early life abandonment, and abuse/neglect issues sustained within their family of origin or with others. Some are additionally affected by alcohol, drug or toxin exposure. These situations all contribute to chemistry changes within the brain, affecting mood and stimulation tolerance.

If a child's thoughts, feelings, or experiences were consistently ignored, that child may use exaggeration, lies, and drama to get the needed attention. Over time, the prefrontal cortex (ability to make healthy decisions by planning with balanced emotions) becomes permanently changed. Due to the new brain circuitry, the child has less ability to stop inappropriate reactions to negative emotions, and he or she acts out instead of managing with healthy strategies.

Procrastination

The fight-or-flight stimulation is also popular among procrastinators who may come to rely on the stimulating effects of sympathetic branch one to complete last-minute projects. Have you ever been in a situation where you had a deadline looming and noticed your anxiety climb as it approached? Do you have an important exam or project to complete for school or work? The night before deadline, as your anxiety peaks, you are flooded with the stimulating effects of fight-or-flight offering you the energy required to complete your tasks. Homemade stress chemical soup is more potent than numerous cups of caffeine, but there is a down side.

Burnout

There *are* consequences for misusing fight or flight. Day after day, this chemical soup release can lead to physical and/or mental health illnesses over time. Some common physical ailments resulting from chronic stress include heart disease, high blood pressure, a greater risk for skin problems, back pain, diabetes, obesity, cancers, and infertility. Section 2 includes the research backing these facts in the comprehensive literature review.

In *Why Zebras Don't Get Ulcers: Third Edition*[19] biologist Robert M. Sapolsky explains that animals like zebras, when chased by a lion, have episodic stress. They rally in the moment, the moment passes, and the stress is over. But for the humans who ruminate on worries of the day, and "what if" of tomorrow, stress is often chronic. This helps explain why many wild animals are less susceptible than humans to chronic stress-related disorders such as high blood pressure, ulcers, endocrine disorders, and cardiovascular diseases.

In addition, a syndrome called *adrenal fatigue* can occur. Overuse of the kidneys' adrenal glands, which release the stress hormones cortisol and adrenaline, can lead to burnout. Overstimulation of your adrenals can occur with a very intense single event or by chronic, repeated stressors that have a cumulative effect.

Cortisol and Belly Fat

If you have struggled with abdominal fat despite your best efforts to exercise and diet, it may be due to the effects caused by cortisol release. This potent chemical soup ingredient is released when the body senses real or your imagined crisis (in your mind), signaling your body to retain belly fat—fuel needed to fight "the danger." Cortisol, a function of primal survival, is concerned with *when our next meal is coming*. It sends the message to reserve and retain belly fat stores. This worked wonders in cave man times when the next meal was never a guarantee, but in our century and country, non-access to food is more the exception than the rule for most. Therefore, chronic cortisol release due to real or imagined stress contributes to abdominal girth increase.

Catching a Cold?

Your stress chemical soup also impacts your immune system. Do you get the cold or flu viruses that skip over those around you? For more information on the immune system and its effects on physical health, refer to the literature review in Section 2.

Memory Issues and Brain Shrinkage

Stephen Stahl has a number of illustrated books with colorful photos that make understanding the complex brain possible. The hippocampal portion in the brain is responsible for short and long-term memory. Decreases in hippocampal volume have been found in patients with long-term post-traumatic stress disorder (PTSD), a condition that develops after experiencing a traumatic event in about seven to eight percent of people exposed.[20]

In PTSD, the brain's chemical soup is turned on with reminders, which cause numbing, intrusive recollections (replaying an event like a movie in your mind), and hyperarousal (overreaction to simple stimuli). Think of these chemicals being released months or years later, as if you were still in the original crisis moment. This creates a track in your brain that possibly carves or sears the memory deeper and affects behavioral responses.

The best personal illustration I can offer to visualize this carving process comes from the seat of a single-engine plane flight over the Grand Canyon. In case you missed it, single-engine means there is no backup in case of failure (yes, adrenaline producing). Looking down on the Colorado River, I could see how the canyon's walls were literally carved from the erosion of its constant flow. Imagine all your thoughts, both positive and negative creating deeper grooves in the brain, affecting how you respond and react in your life. You have the power to deeply entrench either unhealthy or healthy patterns of thought.

Activities designed to help you get off the negative thought trauma tracks and carve different, healthier ones are listed at the end of this section. For most of us, the less time we spend in post-trauma reenactment state, the more likely we are to retain and even *grow* our brain's precious matter. More brain mass means greater functioning and memory.

Take Control of Your Health

In most situations, you will have choices to make about how to manage your own responses. You can choose to ignore the early warning signs and cultivate negative stress effects from your cognitive distortions. Nurturing negative thoughts cause activation of your sympathetic branch one resulting in negative stress effects. Alternatively, you can accept the reality of your current circumstances and summon interventions to call upon your parasympathetic branch two (calms you down) side of the autonomic nervous system. Depending upon the action you take, side one can perpetuate the victim stance and side two, the survivor. In either case, the chemicals generated affect your physical and mental health in the moment and over your lifetime.

My Moment with Actor Brian Dennehy

A few years back, sitting in the second row of a New York City theater, I was mesmerized by the skills of actor Brian Dennehy. He convincingly exuded the negative stress effects of his character, Willy Loman, in *Death of a Salesman*. Sitting so close to the stage, I could literally feel Brian's sweat and spit landing on me as he yelled and flailed his arms. Masterfully, he used his entire body to display emotionally broken Willy's character flaws, including deep anger, unresolved sadness, and frustration for the life he felt a victim to. Dennehy's Tony Award-winning performance was evident as my stomach tightened and my heart pounded faster with each volatile outburst. He was in full fight or flight for most of those few hours as was I, vicariously experiencing Willy's stress through the expert expression of his craft.

When the play ended, my former husband and I were part of a select group invited backstage to meet the famous actor. We exited our row and walked swiftly toward the designated meeting location. Getting ahead of the crowd, I found myself face-to-face with this iconic actor in a nearly empty room. At six foot two, he towered over me, appeared strong and was quite sweaty. His shirt was drenched. While holding a drink in one hand and a cloth in the other to wipe his drippy face and neck, he returned my handshake as I introduced myself.

His ears were purple, and his temple and carotid arteries were throbbing. His breathing was rapid, and I observed him trying to shift gears from the stage to this room, which was soon to be full of admirers like me. Maybe he was even asking himself why he agreed to do this. In either case, he was clearly still fully engaged in fight or flight.

I mustered the courage to ask him the question that had gnawed at me through the entire play: "How in the world do you do that highly emotional performance every day, twice a day, for months and years running straight?"

And he said:

"I must take care of myself, for I am at greater risk for high blood pressure, heart disease, and diabetes because my doctor said that my body doesn't know the difference between my *acting* angry and my actually *being* angry. The result on a cellular level is the same: wear and tear on my body."

What an amazing concept! First of all, in that moment, I developed a deeper appreciation for what actors put themselves through, often at their own expense in their line of duty: fight or flight, negative chemical soup, wear and tear on the body and brain. Returning home, I turned Brian's concept around and came up with another thought that had a powerful impact on my life and private practice.

So, if my body doesn't know the difference between my acting angry or actually being angry (like Brian Dennehy), the result on a cellular level is the same: wear and tear on the body.

Could the reverse be true?

If my body doesn't know the difference between my actually
being on a beach in Hawaii or just imagining I am there,
could the *healing effects* on a cellular level be the same?

Could I learn to heal my body and brain by
eliciting parasympathetic branch two, just by
using my memories and imagination?

Good news! Through my research I found this to be the case.
Let's explore simple and practical strategies for calling on
parasympathetic branch two (calms you down) with more
detail in the next chapter.

PEARL NUMBER EIGHT

CHEMICAL SOUP EFFECTS—HEALING

Branch Two: Parasympathetic

The sympathetic and parasympathetic branches are generally opposites of each other. As explained, the sympathetic branch serves to "jack us up" when faced with a crisis, and the parasympathetic "calms us down." Some refer to parasympathetic branch two activities as "rest and digest" or "feed and breed." The parasympathetic system is designed to conserve energy by slowing the heart rate, decreasing the respiratory rate, increasing intestinal and gland activity, and relaxing the sphincter muscles in the gastrointestinal tract. Branch two is complementary to the other branches and smart enough to take a backseat to branch one during a crisis. Branch two is essential for our healing and occurs when we rest, digest, feed, and breed. Our well-being depends on our ability to learn strategies that call forth branch two and the relaxation response. Section 2 of this book will explore the research and science behind the relaxation response in greater detail.

Returning to the survivor in the sailboat analogy discussed in the fourth pearl of wisdom, let's explore a number of healthy coping strategies that trigger branch two and can be used when faced with any stressful situation.

Healthy Coping Strategies

First, accept the reality of your current stressful situation instead of wasting precious energy fighting against it. Similar to the strategy for being caught in a riptide, it's best to relax into it, and float *with* the current rather than trying to swim against it. In our sailboat analogy, you are stranded without wind, food, and water. Once you accept the facts of your present reality, you can begin the process of problem solving.

The same theory applies to all situations involving relationship challenges. So often we flounder, waiting for a situation or person to change while denying the truth about how our minds and bodies feel when we are with certain people in our work and personal life. Start by accepting your true feelings and responses as others either bring out the best in you, or highlight your flaws as you respond or react to them.

Second, keep the thinking part of your brain (prefrontal cortex) online by taking a series of at least ten deep ujjayi breaths. The ujjayi technique is detailed later in this chapter. You may also consider tapping on a major acupuncture point in your body. To find the spot, place your middle, index, and ring fingers just under your collarbone, and begin rhythmically tapping. This is an effective relaxation tool leading to parasympathetic response, especially when paired with ujjayi breathing. To learn more about tapping, consult Laurel Parnell's book *Tapping In* (2008).[21]

Third, as you are accepting, breathing, and tapping, you intentionally imagine being transported to your calm, peaceful, safe/happy place. Your safe or happy place is any real or imagined location where you feel peaceful and calm. For some of my clients, their safe place is their bed surrounded by soft sheets, blankets, pillows, and pajamas. For others, it may be taking in the view from the top of a special mountain or sitting in a beach chair feeling the warm, gentle ocean water on their toes. If you are struggling with powerlessness, your safe place can be one where you felt powerful at an earlier time in your life. If you struggle with feeling unsafe, your safe place is a location offering you a sense of security. Many therapists warn against putting people in the created safe place, for if they happen to die, it may become a painful trigger versus a helpful aid.

I offer an exception to the "no people" rule, sharing my personal safe place. One of my favorite comforting childhood memories is sitting with my dad in his big leather reclining chair. Snuggled into the crook of his right arm, we would drift off into a peaceful nap while watching *ABC's Wide World of Sports* on a Saturday afternoon. There was no place to go and nothing else to do. Although my father left the earth too soon, I am now more comforted than sad when I conjure up this reclining chair image. Paired with the ujjayi breathing, this is my go-to place whenever I feel anxious or need to keep my prefrontal cortex online.

If your safe place includes other people, the key to its effectiveness lies in being able to sustain the peaceful image in your mind's eye, while feeling relaxed and not triggered by negative emotions such as sadness, anger, frustration, etc. If your safe place creates negative triggers, choose a different option and practice using it anytime you wish to elicit the relaxation and healing effects that parasympathetic branch two offers. Some may argue that no one is truly safe, since danger can occur anytime or anyplace. Therefore a safe *state* versus safe *place* may become the goal for personal affect regulation.

If you are struggling to manage a distressing situation, you might imagine using some kind of *container* such as a locked box, sealed Tupperware or bank vault. As discussed earlier, it is beneficial to change from negative to positive brain thoughts. But in circumstances where you are overwhelmed and struggling to do that, it is often helpful to imagine a way to *lock up* those painful thoughts, images, memories, feelings, emotions, or mind states for periods of time offering you rest. Throughout the day, one by one as they appear, add them to the container. Then when you are ready, you can unlock the container and begin processing at a therapeutic pace either by yourself or with assistance from a great therapist.

Fourth, you may wish to create a *guided imagery* script by visualizing a peaceful scene from a prior adventure or vacation. Are you in the middle of a cold winter season, without a plane ticket to a warm-climate paradise? Here's one option:

Ocean-Guided Imagery Script

Visualize sitting in a canvas sling chair at the ocean's edge. To make this scene more visceral, add tangibility by using all five senses: sight, sound, smell, touch, and taste. Picture the contrasting blues of the water and sky as your eye is drawn to a small boat on the horizon. Overhead you hear the flap of seagull wings. The smell of coconut sunscreen is in the air, as you taste a bit of salt on your tongue. You hear the gentle roar of waves breaking against the white sand as your eyes gaze at the sun's sparkling diamond-like reflections on the shoreline. You reach from your chair and scoop a handful of warm sand feeling the texture and temperature, controlling the slow sift through your fingers. Your toes are caressed by the ebb and flow of the tide as you sink deeper into your chair. You made a purposeful decision to leave your to-do list at home for you are in control of your mind and continue to remain fully focused on this solitary, peaceful place. Choose a cue word now to title your safe place, as if it were a book or movie. Maybe you call it "Bali High" or "Hickory Hills" as you create this new track in your brain. This is your guided imagery video and calling on your cue word can bring this whole scene back anytime you need to feel peaceful and calm, carving out your own positive Grand Canyon memory.

Eye movement desensitization and reprocessing (EMDR) is a powerful intervention and can be used to sear your safe place into the brain and facilitate healing trauma memories. You may consider seeking a therapist trained in EMDR. Dr. Francine Shapiro discovered the well-researched technique in 1987.

Turning on the Protective Immune System

Are you surprised to know that just thinking about the wonderful beach scene described above, with all five senses, activates the parasympathetic branch as the body involuntarily follows the mind? With branch two turned on, your blood pressure and resting heart rate decrease, and your breathing becomes deeper and more even. You begin to digest the breakfast you had a few hours earlier, and you build up your good army of white blood cells. This good army, comprised of lymphocytes and natural killer cells, is on guard to defend against viral and bacterial threats.

To illustrate how your good army (white blood cells) works, let's pretend a small sliver (or splinter) of wood gets under your skin while rowing your boat to shore. Your white cell army immediately recognizes the foreign object and sends its team to the site to gobble up the bacteria present. The eventual swelling creates the counterpressure needed to push the foreign object out of your finger. This miraculous intervention is all part of the white cell army's tactical strategy to keep you healthy.

You may wish to take the time to create your own guided imagery tracks. Begin with one, and create as many as you would like. This simple wellness tool can be called upon throughout the day and over the course of your life to help keep you healthy. Borrow the one offered above or use the following template to begin your own.

Guided Imagery Template

Describe an adventure or vacation:

1. Where are you?
2. What are you doing?
3. What do you *see?*
4. What do you *hear?*
5. What do you *smell?*
6. What are you *touching?*
7. What do you *taste?*

If your mind was engaged and you drifted off to a more peaceful mind-state while doing this exercise, you are on the right path. The more you use your track, the more deeply engrained it becomes, offering you a useful tool whenever you need it.

Brain Growth

In addition to the above autoimmune health benefits, when we utilize all five senses and remain focused on one thing at a time, such as the above guided imagery or our safe, happy place, we are practicing the tenets of mindfulness. Mindfulness has been shown to actually increase certain parts of the brain.

Massachusetts General Hospital studied mindfulness and discovered that mindfulness-based stress reduction practice leads to increases in the brain's gray matter density.[22] Using healthy volunteers, study subjects were given magnetic resonance imaging (MRI) scans before and after they attended the weekly mindfulness classes for eight weeks. The MRI machine uses a magnetic field and radio waves to create detailed images (pictures) of the organs and tissues in the body. During the longitudinal study, researchers compared the before and after images of study participants. At the end of the eight weeks, the participants experienced a 1–3 percent increase in their brain's gray matter within the brain's hippocampus and other regions involved in learning, memory, emotion regulation, and perspective taking.

So if you are interested in improving your memory, enhancing your ability to learn, and increasing emotional stability, develop and utilize mindfulness. Begin with creating your safe, happy place and guided imagery.

"Defragment" the Brain

Think about your brain as a giant computer. If we open up multiple programs all at the same time (numerous thoughts), the system will operate slower. This is especially true as we age or if we use drugs or alcohol to cope. For some, the brain may freeze all together (inability to problem-solve, lack of focus, immobility that comes with panic). But if we regularly defragment our brain like our computer, by powering it down, once rebooted both will perform with greater speed and efficiency. A regular daily practice (begin with just fifteen minutes) including deep breathing, mindfulness, meditation, or guided imagery allows you to power down your brain's computer and facilitate greater performance.

Use a notebook to create your own list of healthy coping techniques. Below are a few ideas to help you get started.

Healthy Coping and Wellness Strategies

1. Ujjayi (ocean-sounding) breathing. Inhale through your nose, filling up your lower abdomen, chest, and back, and then exhale through the back of your throat with your mouth open, making the sound "heeeeer." This stimulates the top of the tenth cranial nerve, which lowers heart and respiratory rate eliciting the parasympathetic branch two *calms you down* side. Use this anytime you need to feel calm. Practice at home first to notice how you are affected. Some people describe feeling lighter or even lightheaded initially. If this is true for you, do not do this exercise while driving or operating machinery. This is the breathing technique used in my doctoral study during the guided

imagery exercise. Practice doing ten to twenty breaths three times a day for a month to create a new habit and use whenever needed.

2. Tapping. Use your index, middle, and ring fingers to tap just below your collarbone thirty times in a row while ujjayi breathing if extra calming effects are needed. Combine breathing and tapping for a powerful strategy for those suffering with anxiety or a panic disorder. This is the first technique I teach clients who have difficulty with airline travel. Combining ujjayi with tapping on the way to the airport, in the bathroom at the airport, and while seated is quite effective. Frequent trips to the plane restroom, during flight, offer an opportunity to stretch, enhancing circulation and privacy while tapping and breathing. This is a powerful initial intervention when you feel yourself beyond a two or three on the anxiety or anger rating scale.

3. Protein snack. Protein helps build muscle and has energy-sustaining power for longer periods of time. The morning egg, protein shake, or almond butter will help keep your blood sugar level through the morning compared to a bagel or sugary cereal that causes a quick blood sugar high followed by the inevitable crash, leaving you tired and hungry.

4. Drink water daily to stay properly hydrated. Water helps balance your immune system, keeps your skin clear by removing toxins, assists with weight management, and increases blood and muscle cells that aid in absorbing nutrients. According to certified sports nutritionist, Jules Hindman of Woburn, Massachusetts, sixteen ounces of chilled water in the morning helps boost metabolism by twenty-four percent. Mayo Clinic and WebMD

offer differing options for daily water calculation. One rule of thumb is eight eight-ounce glasses of water per day provided you are not on a fluid-restricted diet due to health issues. Others recommend multiplying your weight by two-thirds or sixty-seven percent. If you are following the two-thirds rule based on weight, here is a quick calculation guide for you to consider:

Weight	Ounces of Water Daily
100 pounds	67 ounces
110 pounds	74 ounces
120 pounds	80 ounces
130 pounds	87 ounces
140 pounds	94 ounces
150 pounds	100 ounces
160 pounds	107 ounces
170 pounds	114 ounces
180 pounds	121 ounces
190 pounds	127 ounces
200 pounds	134 ounces
210 pounds	141 ounces
220 pounds	148 ounces
230 pounds	154 ounces
240 pounds	161 ounces
250 pounds	168 ounces

5. Walk for twenty minutes. Exercise releases endorphins in your brain, which make you feel good. This may not happen *as* you are exercising, such as "the runners high" (I've not experienced), but know that over time the benefits include lowered depression and improved mood.

6. Engage in any physical activity or sport you enjoy.
7. Time with *safe* family and friends. As mentioned earlier, *safe* people are defined as those whom after you've had contact with, you feel better, versus worse.
8. Play a musical instrument (drumming on the steering wheel during red lights counts). If you have always wanted to learn how to play an instrument, start today. Local music stores offer great prices on used and new instruments with lessons. YouTube video lessons on the Internet offer free quality instructions from the comfort of your home.
9. Take a bath/Jacuzzi. Soaking in warm water boosts your metabolism and relaxes muscles.
10. Write your thoughts/feelings in a journal. James Pennebaker and his colleagues at the University of Texas at Austin studied undergraduate students who experienced a traumatic event.[23] Half of the group was asked to write in a journal about the trauma intermittently over four days. During the same time frame, the remaining half was asked to write about daily activities not including the trauma. Six weeks later, the students who wrote about the trauma reported they felt better and experienced fewer PTSD symptoms than the other group. For many people, the health benefits are immediate. Journaling helps identify feelings and thoughts about your life. This creative and intuitive right-brain activity often unlocks solutions to difficult challenges unveiling new problem-solving strategies. Writing also facilitates the release of intense, painful feelings and emotions, resulting in a calmer, relaxed body and mind. Research on this topic over the

last twenty years reveals great evidence to support the advantages of journaling.

11. Gratitude journal. Create a separate journal to write three things you are grateful for each day as you aim for a thousand. Numerous studies indicate happier mood states are created just from noticing or reframing a negative to a positive. Positive thoughts release neuropeptides that help fight stress and potentially more serious illnesses.

Abraham Lincoln, our late, great sixteenth president of the United States (born 1809, assassinated 1865) captured this negative-to-positive sentiment:

We can complain because rose bushes have thorns, or rejoice because thorn bushes have roses.[24]

In Ann Voscamp's *One Thousand Gifts: A Dare to Live Fully Right Where You Are,*[25] the author shares how she lifted her depression. Setting her personal goal to seek and document a thousand things she is grateful for, Voscamp felt so good when she completed her mission, she started over again. She eloquently illustrates her mental status improvement as she created new tracks in her brain. This process need not be complicated. One simple example: "The elderly man who took a long time picking out the just the right card in the store today."

After reading this book, I was inspired to create my personal gratitude journal. As a survival mechanism, our brains are hardwired to notice the negative first. So given this knowledge, the process of focusing on the positive, may take some practice, but know you are enhancing the perspective on how you view your life.

Consider taking fifteen minutes each day to document at least three personal gratitudes, or positives in your life. This exercise will improve your perspective and mood along with yielding a treasure trove of supportive reminders to reflect upon when you are in need. Don't repeat. Challenge yourself to be creative in your discovery as you begin to look at the whole world differently.

For those of you who have children or a partner, you may wish to adopt the *My Three Things* game. I suggest this strategy to clients in an effort to shift attention away from frightening world events while being nourished as a family. At the dinner table, each member shares three things they are grateful for. Having the expectation to share without repeats sets the stage to begin each day looking for what is *good* and *going right* versus the opposite.

12. Photographs. Take your camera (or camera phone) outside and capture nature. Post or share with others who would appreciate it. Generosity is a mood lifter.
13. Pat animals. They can be yours, others, or those at the local shelter. Research demonstrates the positive effects of human-to-animal interactions. Separate studies by Odendaal[26] and Virues-Ortega[27] indicate that phenylethylamine, a neurotransmitter similar to amphetamine, increased in humans after an interaction of five to twenty-four minutes with their pet. In addition to improved mood, a significant drop in blood pressure also occurred along with lowered cortisol levels and increased immunity. Use of therapy dogs demonstrated a decreased pain perception in postoperative pediatric and adult patients.[28,29] For these reasons, Memorial

Hospital in Belleville, Illinois, created a Family Pet Visitation Policy that allows controlled, safe family cat and dog visitations. After experience with the policy, the nurses concluded it was beneficial for the patient and did not consume excessive amounts of staff time.[30]

My beloved four-pound Toy Poodle *Roxie,* has often been an integral part of my private practice for the past seven years. I am continuously amazed at how she remembers and personally connects with our clients. Depending on their preferences, Roxie either stays out of session, or if joining in, licks only the hands and faces that allow it. By offering her belly to those she trusts, climbing onto laps, or sitting alongside, she provides the extra comfort and support needed. If anger is sensed, she jumps down and heads for the door (very smart animal). She offers her unique brand of therapy, and when the day is done, we are both exhausted but satisfied knowing we provided everything we could to help others.

14. Flower Power. Pick or buy flowers and arrange to your liking. As a child, I enjoyed helping my "memere" arrange silk floral bouquets for our neighbors. They brought special vases or bowls to her and requested a color scheme for upcoming events or holidays. Memere and I "played" together while creating new masterpieces from her endless supply of materials. I didn't know it then, but we were engaging in floral therapy, which calms senses. As an adult, I choose to work with fresh flowers while enhancing my mind and stimulating creativity. There are a variety of techniques, such as ikebana and topiary, or your personal designs. Ikebana, the ancient Japanese art of flower design, focuses on

building closeness with nature. Flowers are arranged with mindfulness and spirituality in quiet, peaceful settings, as the designer appreciates nature.

While many consider floral therapy a method of relaxation, for others it is artistic expression. You may consider learning a few basic guidelines or just see what's in your backyard and let your imagination run wild. Whatever the case, take your time, knowing there is no right or wrong way. If you are enjoying yourself and losing track of time while you create, you are in adult play mode and on the right track.

15. Clean out a closet or drawer. Restoring order and eliminating clutter is liberating and offers a sense of accomplishment and control. Donating slightly used or new items you have not worn in the past year is a great way to give to someone in need.

16. Support local farmers. Drive to your local farm and pick fresh fruit and vegetables, and get busy creating nutritious meals for the day or week.

17. Experiment with food. Find a new recipe and bake a new treat or meal.

18. Create something new. Knit, crochet, embroider, sketch or paint. Your local craft store is filled with instruction, ideas and materials.

19. Fingers in the earth. Plant some flowers in pots or in the ground. Working outside in the soil is grounding and therapeutic.

20. Snooze fest. Take a twenty-minute nap, just long enough to be refreshed but not too long as to interfere with a good night's sleep. Naps are like *snacks* and we want to manage both accordingly.

21. Exercise your funny bone. Watch a hilarious movie and allow yourself to let out a belly laugh until it is hard to catch your breath. If you fall on the floor in hysterics, all the better. Laughter can increase oxygen, which stimulates your heart, lungs, and muscles.

    When was the last time you laughed with abandon? Do you recall how you felt when you stopped to take in more air? Did you feel *high* or find yourself in a relaxed, happier mind state? If so, you were experiencing natural endorphins being released by your brain. These self-made painkillers are also useful for easing discomfort and are all part of our brain's feel-good chemical soup.

22. Interpret your dreams. Our dream state is the subconscious brain's way of trying to share something important about our thoughts and feelings. Sometimes the messages are clear, obvious, concrete, and instructional. Other dreams are designed for emotional healing and may require more effort to unearth the messages. In both cases, distractions of daily life impede the conscious brain's ability to grasp important information. When we dream, the subconscious brain gets to work and begins processing and healing our daily experiences.

    Example one: Concrete problem-solving dream

    Years ago, my former husband was trying to start his car. With the car parked in the driveway of our rented apartment, he lifted the hood, checked the engine, and used jumper cables without success. He spent hours trying to figure out why the vehicle's engine would not turn over. Finally, out of sheer frustration, he gave up and went to bed, still wondering why the engine wasn't getting electricity. The answer came when he dreamed of a particular wire that ran from the starter to the distributor. He woke up, went directly to the vehicle, saw that wire was unattached, connected it, and the car immediately started.

Example two: Emotional healing dream

After my parent's divorce, I was transferred to a new school in the fourth grade. Moving from the familiarity of our family chicken-farm business, surrounded by cousins and grandparents, to the third floor of a triple-decker apartment was anxiety provoking. With the new living arrangements, school change, and ears the size of Dumbo the elephant, I was unaccepted by my peers and teased unmercifully. To my relief, comfort was on its way when one night I had the "flying dream."

In the dream, I stood at the top of the hill outside the new apartment. I began running down the street as fast as I could, and when I picked up enough speed, I extended my arms like airplane wings. The magical moment came when the wind caught my *arm* sails, and I took flight. Lifted off my feet, I soared effortlessly, while joyfully absorbing the aerial vista with a heightened perspective. I felt light and free. No problems or stressors existed as I glided down the hill in a straight line from our apartment to my new school. When I awoke, the peace felt like a healing tonic; it was medicine for my heart, mind, and soul. With my stress effects subdued, I was able to cope at home and school during a challenging time in my life. Before bedtime, throughout those early years, I craved that tonic and prayed God would give me the flying dream. He often did until I was able to be completely free on my own.

As an adult, I can still conjure up those peaceful sensations from my flying dream during a certain yoga pose. The mind is an incredible and fascinating organ. Healthy minds want to heal by returning to homeostasis after stress. Sometimes we just need to get out of the way.

If you would like to learn more about yourself, consider starting a dream diary to capture the messages of your subconscious mind.

This is the format I created for my practice to help glean meaning from dreams:

Dr. Landry's Dream Diary Log Format

It is important to keep the log next to your bed and write as much as possible *immediately* upon waking before the dream becomes a vapor.

Date:

What did you dream about?

Who was in the dream?

What words popped out when you were writing?

Did you identify any symbolism in the dream?

What does the symbolism mean to you?

What were the events of the day or week before?

What were you watching on TV, or what were your thoughts before going to sleep?

What is your interpretation of your dream?

By the time you get to the interpretation section, if you are unable to recognize the meaning, read over your dream and underline words that stand out. Then start at the beginning and read just the underlined words out loud. Often, like a puzzle, the whole picture becomes clear as you have your own *aha!* moments while connecting the dots from your dream to the important message your subconscious is sharing. If you are unable to interpret the message, you will most likely continue to have the same or similar dream. This is especially true of nightmares. Once the message does become clear, the distressing or disturbing dreams usually stop.

To learn more about dream interpretation, consult the works of Sigmund Freud, the father of psychoanalysis, who revolutionized dream analysis. Be wary of quick guides designed like encyclopedias that tell you what your dreams symbolize. Dream interpretation requires your ability to identify what the symbols mean to *you* in relation to personal thoughts and feelings about current or past life events and circumstances. Finding a great therapist with dream analysis interest and experience is a starting place if you are having trouble on your own.

23. Go to a meeting. Find a recovery program and learn to give up and live without addictions in the company of your fellow addicts:

Food: Overeaters Anonymous (OA)

Sex & Love: Sex & Love Addicts Anonymous (SLAA)

Alcohol: Alcoholics Anonymous (AA)

Drugs: Narcotics Anonymous (NA)

Gambling: Gambling Anonymous (GA)

If you or your teens do *not* have a substance addiction but grew up with, or are currently exposed to the direct or indirect effects of alcohol, Al-Anon and Al-Ateen offer wonderful education and support. For relatives and friends of drug addicts, Nar-Anon and Nar-Ateen are invaluable. Local meetings for all these free support/recovery programs are posted on the web and commonly internationally available.

Alcohol Addiction Screening Tool

Have you ever wondered if your alcohol consumption is putting you at risk for alcohol-related problems? Many therapists use the National Institute on Alcohol Abuse and Alcoholism (NIAAA) Guide for Alcohol Screening.

First ask the CAGE questions:

C—Have you ever felt that you should cut down on your drinking?

A—Have people annoyed you by criticizing your drinking?

G—Have you ever felt guilty about your drinking?

> E—Have you ever had a drink first thing in the morning to steady your nerves or get rid of a hangover? (eye-opener).

If you answered yes to any of these above questions, you may be at risk for alcohol-related problems.

To determine the quantity/frequency, ask yourself these questions:

> A. How often? On average, how many days a week do you drink alcohol?
> B. How much? On a typical day, when you drink, how many drinks do you have?

Now multiple A times B for your total. If A is five days a week and B is two drinks on average per day, your total is ten.

For a woman, if you have more than seven drinks a week and for a man, more than fourteen drinks a week, you may be at risk for developing alcohol-related problems.

To determine daily maximum, ask yourself:

How much? What is the maximum number of drinks you had on any given day in the past month?

For a woman more than three and for a man, more than four put you at risk for alcohol-related problems. If you are in this category of risk, consider attending an AA meeting and/or finding a qualified counselor to help you.

24. Daily app use. "The Language of Letting Go" by Melody Beattie (well worth the $6.99) offers daily quick-read messages that focus on codependency and self-care.

25. Set boundaries. Delete or set clear, self-protective boundaries around unsafe "friends" from your Facebook page and your life. Ask yourself, "Do I feel better or worse after having any kind of contact with this person?" If the answer is worse, they are in the unsafe category.

26. Find a great therapist. You can begin by asking your friends for a reference. Thankfully, seeking mental health consultation is now viewed as a healthy, intelligent strategy for good self-care. Friends may not share that information with you unless you ask. They may be seeing a therapist they trust, or know family members or friends who have had positive experiences. In my practice, our first session is about getting to know each other to determine if we are well matched. Understanding this is an emotionally intimate relationship, together we decide if the client feels comfortable and safe with my didactic, direct approach. I also ask myself if I can offer what he *or she* needs based on my expertise and availability or if a colleague would be a better fit. We often have this discussion on intake. In some cases, we part ways based on my decision and/or the client's wishes. This is a very important personal relationship, and it's critical to take the time needed to find the right person to help you. If it's not a good match, give up on the therapist, not on therapy, and keep trying. The same holds true if you've been seeing a therapist for a long time but are not noticing benefits or results. Keep in mind, with all your providers, it is less about the "expert's" ego, and more about getting the best possible care for yourself.

27. Pray/meditate. Engage in your spiritual practice, meditation, or prayer. If you are feeling this void in your life, consult local churches, synagogues, and meditation centers.

28. Eliminate the ANTS. Stop the cognitive distortions and automatic negative thoughts (ANTS). As we discussed, when one ant arrives, the whole troop soon follows. One automatic negative thought often leads to a whole fleet of them, and you begin to swiftly spiral down. Suddenly your mood shifts from content to anxious. What were you thinking just before that occurred? *Stop* the ANTS by distraction, using any number of suggestions on this list, including talking back to the negative thought.

29. Music to my ears. Listen to music. The science behind sound therapy will be explored in greater detail in the dissertation section of this book.

30. Massage therapy. Get a massage from your partner or a professional. Massage therapy increases blood flow, circulation, and endorphins; eases muscle tension; and promotes relaxation. If you are single and not involved in a relationship, professional massage therapy can offer the touch our bodies need to keep our immune system healthy.

31. Offer massage to your loved ones. Generosity boosts endorphins.

32. Read a book. Hard copy or electronic, the choice is yours.

33. Limit caffeine. Caffeine can increase anxiety and trigger the fight-or-flight response, so limit your intake to one or two (eight-ounce) cups a day. One eight-ounce cup of coffee contains 200 mg of caffeine compared to a cup of white tea that has 30 mg. The half-life of caffeine is

a little over five hours. So the 5:00 P.M. coffee is still half in you at 10:00 P.M. and not fully eliminated until 3:00 A.M. Clients often come to therapy with a history of sleeping pill use due to insomnia. Assessment reveals a mid to late afternoon coffee, and all they need to do is substitute the afternoon coffee for a decaffeinated one or a cup of herbal tea. Consider having your last cup of regular coffee at noon to get a good night's sleep.

34. What's going right? Make a list of what is going right in your life. Continue this list by adding your own self-care ideas and actions. By implementing these strategies you are taking action and exercising self-discipline, while enhancing behaviors and thoughts within your control. By focusing on what's right, you build self-efficacy.

PEARL NUMBER NINE

EMBRACE THE CHALLENGE— DEATH PRECEDES REBIRTH

Within Chinese philosophy there is a concept illustrated this way:

Crisis = Disaster + Opportunity

Each crisis offers an opportunity for change and growth. Yin and yang are used to describe how opposite or complementary forces are interconnected. When you choose to see crises as opportunities to evolve, you strengthen your ability to cope and become more empowered. This enriches your life. Each time you decide to be the master of your own destiny, you become "captain of the ship" on this journey called life.

I continue to reinforce that it's not necessarily the crises or the challenges in our lives that determine individual life quality but, more importantly, how we choose to perceive and manage them that guides overall well-being and healthy states of mind and body. How well you can problem-solve and manage life's challenges is a far more important indicator of your physical, spiritual, and mental health and will determine the quality of relationships you will have with others.

One of the most beautiful and encouraging illustrations of finding new life among the ashes of death comes from the giant redwood and sequoia trees in California. Seeds for new growth are found within the cones of these magnificent trees, nearly three hundred feet tall and fifty feet in diameter. The cones are covered with a thick layer of strong resin, which literally glues the cone shut. The only way to open the cones, which allows the release of the two hundred seeds, is by generating enough heat to melt the resin. This is accomplished through planned, accidental, or natural forest fires. The heat melts the resin, the cones break open, and the seeds fall to the earth, landing in the nutrient-rich ashes. Here the seeds have the best possible chance to germinate over the next few years and begin growing into a new tree.

In Elizabeth Lesser's *Broken Open: How Difficult Times Can Help Us Grow* [31] she describes the process of transformation as a journey of brokenness leading to openness, descent to rebirth, and fire to phoenix. In Greek mythology, a phoenix is a long-lived bird that is regenerated or reborn. The phoenix obtains new life by rising from the ashes of its predecessor. Revel in the crisis for new life is coming.

Along the way, know that difficult journeys are best taken in a strong vehicle, or at least with a trusted guide and a helpful toolbox. The practices Lesser shares during her phoenix times include prayer, meditation, and psychotherapy, which enable her to keep both mind and heart open. Prayer offers solace and strength while meditation keeps the heart steady and the mind less agitated and reactive. Psychotherapy enables her to see the cause and effect while moving closer toward taking personal responsibility for happiness, rather than waiting for someone or something else to fix or define her life.

Personally, my deepest growth has come from the "fire times" in my life. Those are the remarkable and profoundly dark places we try to avoid at all costs in a variety of ways.

But only when we stop the denial and face the truth can we begin the slow burn that eventually leads us to drop new seeds into that nutrient-rich soul soil. Eventually those seedlings sprout with newfound awareness and wisdom leading us on to a higher place.

In this first section, I offered useful pearls of wisdom for your self-help tool collection and hopefully shed light on the path from pain to growth. The next section contains my complete doctoral dissertation on the effects of Himalayan singing bowl therapy. You may notice a distinctive change in writing style for documentation of research is less personal than writing for sharing. Concepts are often repeated more frequently. Section 2 offers access to the valuable research and evidence results from the study, along with a number of useful references for personal knowledge and a template for those who may wish to conduct a similar themed project. Use the next section as it best suits your personal learning needs. If you get overwhelmed in the subject density, don't fear, as I have summarized the entire research study in Section 3, using the more user-friendly writing style of Section 1.

SECTION 2

DOCTORAL DISSERTATION

Doctoral Dissertation

MEASURING THE EFFECTS OF A HIMALAYAN SINGING BOWL ON A MEDITATION PRACTICE: A QUANTITATIVE APPROACH by Jayan M. Landry

THOMAS PAGE Ph.D., Faculty Mentor and Chair GARY SZIRONY Ph.D., Committee Member, EDWARD BELL Ph.D., Committee Member

David Chapman, Psy.D., Dean, Harold Abel School of Social and Behavioral Sciences

© Jayan Landry, 2012

Abstract

The stress response in certain situations offers many benefits including sharpened focus, increased energy and alertness for academic, business/athletic performance, and critical fight or flight reactions necessary for survival. Life in our society predisposes us to stressful events with most individuals managing while maintaining optimum health. However, some circumstances beyond our control can overwhelm innate responses, as cumulative stress effects take a toll on emotional and physical well-being. Effective providers need access to empirical data describing interventions to improve health and overall functioning. This quantitative study was designed to determine physiological and psychological effects of adding Himalayan singing bowl (HSB) exposure prior to a directed relaxation (DR) session. Research questions and hypotheses aimed to determine relaxation effects (Positive and Negative Affect States – [PANAS]) and physiological responses (blood pressure [BP] and heart rate [HR]) to HSB exposure prior to a DR. Fifty-one adult female and male participants attended two sessions within a one-month time period. Study sessions were randomly assigned to have HSB exposure or silence prior to DR session. There was a positive relationship between HSB exposure, physiological and relaxation responses evidenced by a significantly greater decline in systolic BP and HR with HSB when compared to silence alone. Decreases in diastolic BP were greater in the HSB group with a non-significant trend. Hypertensive individuals ($n = 20$) had significant changes from baseline in both systolic and diastolic BP when compared to normotensives ($n = 31$) at first and second measurements. Fifty of fifty-one participants reported feeling more relaxed at the end of both sessions and indicated positive associations with HSB exposure (deeper meditative state, enhanced spiritual experience, ocean imagery). Building upon prior research in relaxation and sound in Eastern and Western practices, this study offers innovative approaches to stress management evidenced by decreases in systolic and diastolic BP, HR, and negative affect states when incorporating HSB into a meditation session. Results will have broad implications in the wider psychology and mental health fields offering clinicians practical tools for assisting clients with stress management.

SECTION TWO

CHAPTER 1

INTRODUCTION

Introduction to the Problem

Most of us live in a world filled with daily stressful events and are challenged by a number of demands. Many individuals will cope in healthy ways by managing or overcoming these issues, and they will not result in disease conditions. Others will experience events as stressors, and without beneficial coping strategies, they can evolve into a series of uncomfortable symptoms disrupting the ability to lead a productive, healthy, and happy life. These symptoms can manifest as anxiety or depression and have a negative impact on the physical, mental and spiritual quality of life. Individuals often present for therapy seeking relief and assistance for their discomfort. Comprehensive client management requires an approach that encompasses the physical, mental, and spiritual realms of functioning. As mental health care providers, we are challenged to discover and implement strategies that could enhance the relaxation response, proven to assist with stress management while alleviating anxiety and depressive symptoms (Benson 1975, Bjerklie et al., 2003). Knowing, that part of the human condition involves being subjected to stressful events, we understand stress can be considered 'the great equalizer' since few are immune and stress does not discriminate based on socioeconomic, demographic or geographic factors. One helpful approach involves embracing stress and viewing it as a natural part of life. This allows us to explore, in a number of ways, our understanding and management of effective, healthy and non-costly interventions. Research has been revealing the efficacy of Eastern approaches as a complement to our Western culture in the area of stress management. It is imperative we continue to examine additional facets in an effort to enhance our knowledge base and contribute to the field of complementary and alternative management approaches CAM.

We will be exploring a number of strategies that could enhance the established relaxation response, which has proven to complement stress management (Benson, 1975), and alleviate anxiety and depressive symptoms (Bjerklie et al., 2003). Dr. Herbert Benson (1975) was one of the first medical doctors to discover the *Relaxation Response* when he objectively measured the relationship between stressful psychological events and the associated physiological changes affecting one's health. Dr. Benson is a pioneer in the field of mind/body medicine. Throughout his thirty-five year career, he defined the relaxation response and continues to research its efficacy in counteracting the harmful effects of stress. His work offers us a bridge between Eastern and Western medicine and religion, in the field of mind/body, belief and science.

Over the decades since Benson's work, a number of complementary and alternative methods, including effects of sound therapy on stress management have emerged. There is a plethora of medical, mental health and complementary medicine practitioners who have studied the positive physiological effects of music, sound, and vibration spanning the centuries (Adero, 2001; Gass & Brehony, 1999; Gaynor, 1999; Goldman, 2008; and Halpern, 1977). Specifically, Himalayan singing bowls HSB have been used for ceremonial and meditation purposes, and are being used by practitioners to enhance relaxation and meditation (Huyser, 1999).

As meditation has become demystified over the decades and mainstreamed as a therapeutic technique, there remains a nugget of Buddhist philosophy: sitting in silence for ten to forty minutes a day while concentrating on breath, word or an image, facilitates *presence* and a more relaxed mind and body (Bjerklie et al., 2003). This study attempted to improve upon Bensons' (1975) relaxation response by determining if introducing a Himalayan singing bowl prior to a meditation session would promote an enhanced relaxation response.

Stress hormones such as cortisol and adrenaline are useful when needed in a true crisis when "fight or flight" is required for survival. However, medical problems develop when one lives their life in this chronic stress state. These psychosocial stressors and stress hormones can lead to hypertension (Weiner, 1977) cardiac disease (Hanser, 1985), gastrointestinal problems (Khorana, 1983), and migraines (Steven & Shanahan, 2002). It is imperative to continue exploring preventive measures to enhance positive physiology thereby limiting the impact these stressors can have on illness causation.

Transcendental Meditation (TM) has been shown to have a positive effect on lowering blood pressure. A study of hypertensive African Americans, who were exposed to TM for twenty minutes twice daily, indicated a decrease in blood pressure -3/-5 mm Hg over twelve months (Schneider et al., 2005). In addition, Paul-Labrador et al. (2006) discovered in a randomized trial of TM in comparison to health education in patients with coronary heart disease, TM showed significant benefits on blood pressure (-3/-2mm Hg) and insulin resistance over a sixteen-week period.

Within the field of CAM, this researcher attempted to determine if adding HSB exposure prior to a meditation session had positive effects on physiology. The results will have broad ramifications in the field of mental health counseling. Depending on study results, practitioners would have the option of adding HSB exposure to a relaxation session with the knowledge it may enhance the client's positive physiology in both physical and mental health realms. This research will advance best practices in the field of meditation and relaxation improving mental and physical well-being in the clients we serve.

Statement of the Problem

The body of empirical evidence proving the mind-body connection, and the negative effects of stress on our health is growing. The ramifications of anxiety and stress on mental health have been widely recognized. Numerous experts estimate up to seventy-five percent of fatigue and medical disorders are directly attributable to stress (Hughes, Pearson, & Reinhart, 1984; Kaptein, Van der Ploeg, Carseen, & Beunderman, 1990).

Since stress hormones play such an essential role in determining one's mental and physical well-being, it is crucial to continue exploring alternative preventative measures before stressors overwhelm the body and evolve into serious medical conditions. Since it was unknown if adding HSB to a directed meditation practice will demonstrate a positive physiological and psychological response, this research project offers an important contribution in the area of stress reduction and management.

Purpose of Study

The purpose of the study was to discover the physiological and psychological effects of adding HSB exposure prior to a directed relaxation session. This researcher, a licensed therapist in private practice is motivated and inspired to determine HSB effects on physiology and affect. The concept of combining Eastern and Western approaches when working with clients exhibiting stress related disorders is intriguing.

Research Questions

The primary research question (1) and sub questions (2-3) in this study:

1. What are the physiological and relaxation effects when integrating HSB exposure prior to a directed relaxation DR session?
2. Will the HSB produce an enhanced effect on blood pressure and pulse rate when added prior to DR session versus no HSB exposure prior to a meditation session?
3. Will there be an enhanced relaxation experience measuring positive and negative affect (PANAS rating scale) with HSB exposure prior to a directed relaxation session as opposed to no HSB exposure prior to directed relaxation session?

Directional Hypothesis

Directional Hypothesis: There is a positive relationship between the use of HSB exposure and enhanced relaxation along with positive physiological effects when used prior to DR.

Rationale, Relevance, and Significance of the Study

Rationale for Study

This topic is important to study for it is known that emotional stress often leads to physical and emotional dis-*ease*. Clinicians seeking stress management options, will have an additional tool, enabling them to offer the highest standard of care in the field of relaxation and stress reduction. With an estimated seventy-five percent of fatigue and medical disorders being directly related to stress and anxiety (Hughes et al., 1984; Kapstein et al., 1990), the scientific community is challenged to discover interventions to reduce stress.

Since complementary and alternative methods CAM are new in the field of relaxation response, credible scientific research studies are needed to examine and test the validity and reliability of claims made by practitioners that HSB use is effective in relaxation promotion. It is important to examine the specific physiological effects of sound and vibration. Many practitioners note personal positive experiences with sound and vibration (Adero, 2001; Gass, 1999; Gaynor, 1999; Goldman, 2008; Halpern, 1977), but little empirical data exists studying the direct effects on affect, blood pressure and heart rate when exposed to HSB.

Himalayan singing bowls are interesting for they have been used over the years in ceremonial and meditation purposes to enhance relaxation (Huyser, 1999). There is a paucity of empirical data determining the effect on systolic and diastolic blood pressure, heart rate and subjective relaxation effects using instruments such as the self-administered PANAS tool. Given the lack of prior research and published findings determining the effects of adding HSB exposure to a directed relaxation session, this study was essential.

Relevance of the Study

As therapists and mental health providers, we are charged with the responsibility of offering the highest standard of care to our clients. Each clinical challenge offers the clinician the opportunity to implement best practices. With stress management being a crucial cornerstone for mental and physical well-being, the study offered new information on best practices regarding utilization of HSB exposure along with a relaxation session. Results from this study will make a significant contribution to scientific research by advancing theories and extending knowledge within the relaxation response field.

Significance of the study

Study results will significantly contribute to the body of knowledge within the scientific community in the area of relaxation response, sound, vibration and music as therapy. Results have the power to change best practices as clinicians assist themselves and their clients with effective relaxation options. They may introduce for the first time, the utilization of HSB exposure prior to a meditation session when attempting to enhance the relaxation response armed with the knowledge that HSB inclusion enhances positive physiology. Greater stress management improves physical and mental well-being offering the potential to result in a higher quality of life. Building on this concept, this project will spur further research in the area of sound and vibration, impacting relaxation and stress management.

With debate among bowl practitioners; metal versus crystal, similar studies using different bowls with alternate sizes could be compared. Other experiments, using the same size and tone HSB used for this study, but made of crystal versus metal would be interesting. Perhaps future experiments could be conducted using specific bowl tones that correspond directly with the chakras in need of support. Chakras will be explained in more detail in Chapter 2. Knowledge gained from this research project will advance best practices in the field of meditation and relaxation while improving mental and physical well-being in the clients we serve.

Nature of the Study

The researcher proposed a quantitative correlational design to answer the research questions; how does adding HSB (potential stress reduction tool) prior to directed relaxation session effect physiological reactions and subjective relaxation states? The experiment was based on defined variables and had a finite time frame to establish cause and effect. The independent variable is the HSB. The dependent variable is the meditation session. This research experiment used a sample size of fifty-one male and female adult participants within a fifty-mile radius of a suburban Boston community in Massachusetts.

Whenever large numbers of participants are needed, a convenience sample is justified (Creswell, 2009). The design is created to compare the two conditions with no random assignment, for the individual will serve as their own control in an effort to minimize variables. Sampling strategy utilized convenience sampling with flyers posted in local downtown public places including the library, medical offices, senior center, bookstores and markets within a fifteen-mile radius of the research location.

Over the past thirty years, systolic blood pressure measurements, have been used by Benson (1975) and Bjerklie et al. (2003), as a valid means to test the relaxation response. This study included quantifiable data from physiological measurements (blood pressure, pulse) and supplemental qualitative data taken from researcher-administered relaxation rating scale (PANAS). The reliabilities of the PANAS scales, as measured by Cronbach's alpha, were .89 for PA and .85 for NA. The narrowness of the confidence limits associated with these coefficients indicate they can be regarded as providing very accurate estimates of the internal consistency of the PANAS in the general adult population. Thus, both PA and NA scale can be viewed as possessing adequate reliability (Crawford & Henry, 2004).

PANAS has been used to effectively measure positive and negative affect states in a number of research studies. Clinical improvements were evaluated using PANAS scores in patients with deep brain stimulation for treatment-resistant depression (Mayberg et al., 2005). Positive and negative affect states were measured with PANAS along with associated mindfulness with rock climbers (Steinberg, 2011) and bungee jumpers (Middleton, Harris & Surman, 1996). Lord and Menz (2002) used PANAS to assess mobility, physical functioning and overall cardiovascular fitness after incorporation of a six-minute walk program for older adults. Health–risk behavior in adolescents correlated with increasing emotional response to music when PANAS was used in Roberts, Dimsdale, East and Friedman's (1998) study. As in this study, when there is a desire to accurately measure positive and negative affect states, the PANAS has been proven to be a valid and reliable tool.

Definition of Terms

Does adding a Himalayan Singing Bowl HSB (potential stress reduction tool), prior to directed relaxation DR session affect the physiological (blood pressure and pulse) and emotional state (PANAS) of adults?

Himalayan Singing Bowls HSB - The bowl used in this study is from Nepal. Bowls from this region have been traditionally used for ceremonial and meditation purposes, and are handcrafted using alloys of several metals to produce different tones, depending on composition, shape, size and weight (Inacio, 2004). To control for as many variables as possible, it was important to determine the tone of this particular study bowl. When rubbed and struck using the impacting stick called a puja, the six-inch metal HSB was determined (by musician John Bermani using a Petersen Strobe Tuner), to be vibrating around a B^b pitch.

Directed Relaxation DR - This consisted of a prerecorded twenty-minute audio relaxation session (see appendix for script) recorded on the researcher's IPAD. All participants listened to the same twenty-minute audio recording at the end of both sessions.

HSB Session - The bowl was played immediately before the DR session by the investigator for a total of twelve minutes alternating striking the bowl until the sound trails off (approximately thirty seconds) for the first minute and then rubbing with the puja for the second minute. This mode and length of time offers the best exposure to bowl sound (Mitch Nur, PhD, personal communication, July 15, 2011).

Silence session - The participant was asked to get comfortable and the researcher left the room for twelve minutes.

Puja - The wooden exciting stick with one side covered in soft leather used to produce sound from the bowl by impacting or rubbing the rim and side of the bowl.

Blood pressure and heart rate measurements – An automatic blood pressure cuff device (IntelliSense manufactured by Omron, Model # HEM-747IC) was used to obtain and record preset interval data (blood pressure and heart rate) offering reliable numerical scores. Session measurements included: systolic/diastolic blood pressure and heart rate. These were taken pre-session, repeated after the twelve minutes of either silence or HSB intervention and a third time after the twenty-minute DR.

Relaxation effect -

A. The participant was asked if there were any new stressful events in their lives when they returned for the second session within two weeks of the first session.
B. Participants completed the Positive and Negative Affect Scale (PANAS) pre and post session.
C. Participants were asked if they felt more relaxed at the end of session compared to the beginning.

Assumptions and Limitations

The researcher predicted there would be a decrease in blood pressure and heart rate along with an increased participant evaluated relaxation state after the session that included the HSB exposure prior to the directed relaxation compared to the silence session. It was thought that the parasympathetic nervous system would react favorably to the sound and vibration of HSB, and be reflected by the participant having more positive versus negative affect, as measured by the PANAS rating scale. In addition, it was believed that blood pressure would be significantly decreased, and pulse slightly decreased, indicating a deeper state of relaxation within the physical body. The participant serving as their own control eliminates variables that could hinder result reliability. Serial blood pressure and pulse monitoring with an automatic blood pressure cuff offered consistent measurements without disruption to the relaxation state. The participant was retested with the PANAS scale at the beginning and end of session thereby ensuring rater validity and reliability.

Complementary and alternative medicine techniques to lower blood pressure have been evaluated although limitations and biases are present in many studies. In a study that directly compared Tai Chi to resistance training among healthy elderly participants over a twelve-month period, there was no significant effect of Tai Chi on blood pressure (Thomas et al., 2005). However, a systematic review of the health outcomes of Tai Chi revealed there did appear to be physiological and psychological benefits (Wang, Collet, & Lau, 2004).

Stress reduction through transcendental meditation (TM) has had varied effects on blood pressure. Results of a meta-analysis of randomized trials of TM revealed no convincing evidence for an effect of TM on blood pressure, with significant concerns about study methodologies and potential author bias.

The dual role of researcher and facilitator produces a limitation. The natural subjectivity of reporting could be reflective in the findings. The sample size was a mixture of gender and ages from one affluent Boston suburban community therefore assumptions drawn may have bias and not be applicable to the general population. In addition, the sample size is moderate (fifty-one) and the researcher's choice of bowl size and tone while pleasing to her may not be to all participants.

CHAPTER 2

LITERATURE REVIEW

Introduction

The focus of this research was to determine if adding the sound and resonance of a Himalayan singing bowl HSB will have a measurable effect on the central nervous system prior to a twenty-minute directed relaxation DR session. Physiological effects were measured by comparing pre and post session blood pressure and heart rate with and without a twelve-minute HSB exposure prior to a DR session. Perceived relaxation effects were measured utilizing the positive and negative affect scale (PANAS) pre and post session. This chapter will discuss the theoretical framework for the study and present a thorough literature review of previous research related to this topic.

Theoretical Framework Relaxation and the Mind-Body Connection

The components of the theoretical framework for the study include the relaxation response, and research findings associated with improved health via stress management using meditation, and exposure to sound and vibration. The instruments measured diastolic/systolic blood pressure, and heart rate along with positive and negative affect traits as reported by participants. The dependent measures of interest were the changes in the parasympathetic nervous system, responsible for decreasing blood pressure, and heart rate when inducing the *relaxation response*. In addition, there was an analysis of the positive and negative effects using the PANAS scale to determine the psychological effects as rated by the participant. The framework chosen is based on Herbert Benson's (1975) *relaxation response* model.

In 1975, Dr. Herbert Benson, a professor of medicine at Harvard Medical School published his ground breaking book *The Relaxation Response*. Benson was able to demonstrate the direct relationship between stressful psychological events and the associated physiological changes affecting one's health. Based on research from a decade earlier, he studied thirty-six transcendental meditators (TM) and found when they meditated, they used seventeen percent less oxygen, lowered their heart rates by three beats a minute, and had an increase in theta brain waves (Bjerklie et al., 2003). He therefore concluded the meditators counteracted the stress-induced fight-or-flight response and achieved a calmer, happier state. His findings were a significant contribution to the field of relaxation and the mind-body connection.

Musical Effects on the Brain and Body

According to legend, Pythagoras (c. 570-c. 495 BC), a Greek philosopher and mathematician contributed to early theories of music and sound. He noted healing effects of music in his community when people listened to the hammering sounds produced by blacksmiths. This compilation of sounds inspired him to develop harmonic theories and musical scales while conducting research on his lyre. He experimented by stretching strings of equal tension to discover the underlying mathematics of the musical scale. A string producing a C note, stretched twice its length will also produce a C, but resonate an octave lower in a 2:1 ratio. Other notes can be obtained by taking simple fractions of the string with 3/2:1 = 3:2 producing an F; and 4/3:1 = 4:3 producing a G (Prochazka, 2004). Pythagoras believed that music and mathematics were linked and everything in the universe was a series of harmonies. He played his lyre to infuse his own soul with divine qualities and played for others believing that music possessed spiritual and healing properties. When Pythagoras played, he experienced deeper relaxation and witnessed greater well-being for those suffering from physical and mental ailments (Gaynor, 1999).

In conclusion, by measuring the physical and emotional effects of incorporating both meditation and sound, this study tests, refines and advances these two theories. As part of the analysis and interpretation of collected data through blood pressure, pulse and PANAS scores, the researcher examined and explained the findings in light of assumptions and theoretical expectations by extending the body of knowledge in the area of relaxation response theory associated with sound and vibration.

Review of Critical Literature

Scientific Discoveries

The Brain's Positive Response To Meditation

There are a number of meditation techniques available including transcendental meditation TM, guided imagery, directed relaxation, mindfulness meditation, and singing bowl. It would be a mistake to assume each technique produces the same results; therefore, it is necessary to examine each procedure and resulting response separately. From a scientific perspective, one considers the concept that different techniques will produce different results in terms of outcome variables (blood pressure, heart rate, stress levels, brain immunity, EEG, etc). As such, they need to be evaluated individually.

Orme-Johnson and Walton (1998), revealed in their meta-analyses, transcendental meditation TM was more effective in reducing anxiety, drug abuse, alcohol abuse, and cigarette use when compared to other forms of meditation, relaxation, and health promotion. In addition, TM indicated a more effective increase in self-actualization compared to other meditation, relaxation techniques and standard treatments. The positive outcomes were attributed to the enhanced relaxation state the transcendental meditation program produced.

Direct physiological effects on brain wave reactions have been measured after implementing another form of meditation- the Relaxation Response (RR). In an effort to pinpoint specifically how relaxation affects the human brain, Gregg, Jacobs, and Benson (1996) studied how the central nervous system reacts when exposed to RR effects. In their controlled study using novice subjects, topographic EEG mapping was established as their dependent measure. Twenty subjects listened to RR and control audiotape presented in a counterbalanced order while EEG patterns were recorded from fourteen scalp locations. The RR condition produced greater (p<.0164) reductions in frontal EEG beta activity relative to the control condition. No significant differences were observed for any other frequency band or scalp region. Their findings suggested that elicitation of the RR produced significant reductions in cortical activation in anterior brain regions in novice subjects.

In addition to meditation effects on EEG brain wave patterns, TM impacts cerebral blood flow. Newburg, Pourdehnad, and O'Aquili (2003) studied cerebral blood flow during a verbal meditation offered to a group of Franciscan nuns. The meditation was fifty minutes long. Subjects repeated a particular phrase consistent with teachings of transcendental meditation TM. Findings revealed a 7.1 % increased blood flow in the subject's prefrontal cortex. Results are relevant as this specific brain area is responsible for cognitive processing. One may conclude that TM improves brain functioning in the locations associated with storing knowledge, thinking, and memory functions (Newburg et al., 2003).

Complementary to the TM approach, which proved to have positive effects on electrical brain activity and blood flow, mindfulness meditation was put to the test to measure brain immune function. Davidson et al., (2003) performed a randomized controlled study using twenty-five healthy employees in their work environment. Their well-known widely used eight-week clinical training program in mindfulness meditation was tested. Electrical brain activity was measured before, immediately after employees were taught mindfulness meditation, and then four months following the eight-week training. A wait-list control group ($n = 16$) was tested at the same points in time as the meditators. At the end of the eight-week period, subjects in both groups were then vaccinated with the influenza vaccine. Results revealed the meditator group had significant increases in left-sided anterior activation (a pattern previously associated with positive affect) when compared to the non-meditators. In addition, researchers found significant increases in antibody titers to influenza vaccine among subjects in the meditation group compared to those in the wait-list control group. The magnitude of increase in left-sided activation predicted the magnitude of antibody titer rise to the vaccine. Their findings demonstrated a short program in mindfulness meditation produced demonstrable, positive effects on brain and immune function, essential for mind-body health.

Stress reduction through transcendental meditation TM has also been shown to affect blood pressure. In a study of hypertensive African Americans, TM for twenty minutes twice daily resulted in a decrease in blood pressure -3/-5 mm Hg over twelve months (Schneider et al., 2005). Their long-term follow up study of participants in trials using TM versus other behavioral stress reducing interventions, found the TM group had a twenty-three percent reduction in all-cause mortality and a thirty percent reduction in cardiovascular mortality. Therefore, stress-reducing interventions such as TM may have beneficial effects among individuals with hypertension (Schneider et al., 2005).

Supporting Schneider et al.'s (2005) work, Paul-Labrador et al. (2006) demonstrated the relationship between TM and its beneficial effects on blood pressure. Their study included a randomized trial of TM in comparison to health education in patients with coronary heart disease. Results revealed significant benefits on blood pressure (-3/-2mm Hg) and insulin resistance over a sixteen-week period (Paul-Labrador et al., 2006).

More recently, nine randomized controlled trials met eligibility criteria for a meta-analysis of TM effects on blood pressure (Anderson, Liu & Kryscio, 2007). The random effects meta-analysis model for systolic and diastolic blood pressure indicated transcendental meditation, compared to controls, was associated with: -4.7 mm Hg (95% confidence interval (CI), -7.4 to -1.9 mm Hg and -3.2 mm Hg (95% CI, -5.4 to -1.3 mm Hg). Subgroup analyses of the hypertensive groups and high quality studies showed similar reductions. Authors concluded the regular practice of transcendental meditation, may have the potential to reduce systolic and diastolic blood pressure by 4.7 and 3.2 mm Hg respectively, representing clinically meaningful changes.

An alternative complementary medicine technique such as Tai Chi has been hypothesized to lower blood pressure. Efforts to measure Tai Chi's effect on blood pressure have been evaluated although limitations and biases are present in many studies. In a systematic review of the health outcomes of Tai Chi, there appear to be physiological and psychological benefits (Wang et al., 2004).

The Relaxation Response RR is characterized by decreased oxygen consumption, increased exhaled nitric oxide, and reduced psychological distress (Benson, 1975). Three decades later, Dusek et al. (2008) advanced the RR theory by hypothesizing RR elicitation results in characteristic gene expression changes that can be used to measure physiological responses of RR in an unbiased fashion. Researchers assessed whole blood transcriptional profiles in nineteen healthy, long-term practitioners of daily RR practice (group M), nineteen healthy controls (group N1), and 20 N1 individuals who completed eight weeks of RR training (group N2). Two thousand two hundred and nine genes were differentially expressed in group M, relative to group N1 ($p<0.05$) and 1561 genes in group N2 compared to group N1 ($p<0.05$). Importantly, 433 ($p<10-10$) of 2209 and 1561 differentially expressed genes were shared among long-term (M) and short-term practitioners (N2). Analyses revealed significant alterations in cellular metabolism, oxidative phosphorylation, generation of reactive oxygen species and response to oxidative stress in long-term and short-term practitioners of daily RR practice. These effects may counteract cellular damage related to chronic psychological stress. This study provides the first compelling evidence that RR elicits specific gene expression changes in short-term and long-term practitioners relative to long-term physiological effects (Dusek et al., 2008).

Along with Dusek et al. (2008), additional researchers in the past decade have studied DNA microarray technology allowing for the expression level measurement of many thousands of genes. This information offers concrete and objective contributions to the mind body field. New experimental options have revolutionized research in the area of molecular biology and serve as a template for individualized medical approaches (Eisen, Spellman, Brown, & Botstein, 1998).

Researchers have documented the use of DNA microarrays for assessing therapeutic responses to psychological relaxation and meditative practices on the molecular-genomic level (Dusek et al., 2008; Rossi, 2002, 2004, 2005, 2007). This growing body of research substantiates psychotherapy, pastoral counseling, psychiatry, and therapeutic hypnosis offering a positive *top down* response from mind to gene (Rossi, 1986, 1993, 2007; Rossi & Rossi, 2008). Rossi's (2008) most recent experimental design research using three subjects focused on the possible role of therapeutic hypnosis using their *Creative Psychosocial Genomic Healing Experience*. Using DNA microarray analysis, results indicated a response to the therapeutic protocol within one hour after the treatment through the expression of fifteen early response genes up-regulated between 1.2 and 1.8 folds with no single gene being down-regulated. A further cascade of seventy-seven genes occurred twenty-four hours later. Researchers concluded additional studies would be required for cross validation using a larger sample size in order to document the validity and reliability of using DNA microarrays to assess their therapeutic protocol (Rossi, 2008).

Additional Pathways to Positive Brain/Body Physiology

It is imperative to expand prior research and build evidence for best practices, by exploring additional avenues for enhanced mental and physical response to meditation. Researchers may consider the specific effects sound has on health. Do the vibrations of singing, sound exposure, prayer, or chanting effect physiology and the relaxation response? Vilayat (1982) extolled the virtues of chanting within the Sufi ritual. Chanting vowels to hear various harmonics and the mixture of tones is part of Sufi tradition, allowing for healing power generated from the sounds created. Can this be measured more comprehensively?

Emoto (2004) researched the sound and vibrational effects on water droplet configurations. He suggests, since humans are seventy percent water, we will be highly affected as our cell shape responds to tone, vibration and composition of sound. In his experiments, when the round water droplet (representing our cells) was exposed to heavy metal music, using a black background microscope, the edges became erratic. In contrast, when the round drop was exposed to classical music, the edges became more symmetrical-even snowflake shaped. Critics of Emoto's (2004) work assert he had insufficient experimental controls, and neglected to share critical details of his research approach within the scientific community. Tiller (2005), critiques Emoto designed experiments in ways leaving them open to human error, which could have influenced his findings. Either way, Emoto offers compelling photographs of his work *Hidden Messages in Water,* illustrating the cellular impact of sound and vibration.

Contrasting the topic of cell effects with external music, how does singing impact cellular response and physical health? Adero's (2001) research was consistent with his theory that singing is good for your lungs. His study examined the specific effects singing had on the lung capacity of patients at the University Hospitals of Cleveland-Ireland Cancer Center. Results indicated patients who sang exhibited improvements in respiratory conditions including pneumonia and bronchial ailments requiring sufficient lung oxygenation. Thus, singing was determined to be a natural and effective method for increasing oxygen flow through lung capacity expansion (Adero, 2001).

If singing increases oxygen by expanding lung capacity, could the vibrations that accompany singing have additional effects on physiology? Gass and Brehony (1999) were able to support this concept with their research. Vibration is the physical motion, which accompanies singing, chanting, speech and vocal prayer. Their study, based on clinical practice, points to the power of vibration, which appears to charge brain cells, lower blood pressure and balance heart rhythm. These positive effects induced relaxation and resulted in mood elevation (Gass

& Brehony, 1999). Similarly, Halpern (1977) researched the effects his music had on healing. He discovered connections between sound and healing by demonstrating positive brainwave patterns utilizing biofeedback and aura photography.

Based on prior research regarding the healing effects of sound, there is no "one size fits all" approach. Individuals seem to exhibit personal musical preferences (Goldman, 2008). Seashore (1937) underscores that concept through his work revealing how specific musical compilations affect the psyche of individuals. He demonstrated forty percent of his subjects enjoyed a specific piece of music they personally chose, while the other forty percent disliked it. The remaining twenty percent remained neutral-neither liking, or disliking it. Goldman's (2008) book "The Seven Secrets of Sound Healing," explores the concept of vibrational science in greater detail. He outlines the relevant sound concepts including: vibration, intention, uniqueness, silence, voice as healing instrument, notes in the scale, and the power of sound as a change agent.

Dynamics of the Himalayan Singing Bowl

Inacio (2004) and Nur (2011) offered clinical perspectives on how to play the HSB with efficacy and with a standardized sequencing. Their experience was considered when creating the HSB session for this study. Tibetan bowls have been traditionally used for ceremonial and meditation purposes. Bowls are handcrafted, often using alloys of several metals, which produce different tones, depending on their composition, shape, size and weight (Inacio, 2004). Sound, is created by impacting or rubbing the side of the bowl with the exciting stick (called puja) frequently made of wood and covered with a soft skin on one end (Jansen, 1993). Singing bowls, designed by

Himalayans or Nepalese (Gaynor, 1995, 2002) are traditionally made in Tibet, Nepal, Bhutan, Mongolia, India, China and Japan. The alloys may include – mainly copper and tin, but some have gold, silver, iron, and lead. Each are believed to possess particular spiritual powers. The HSB utilized for this study, originated in Nepal, was purchased by Mitch Nur and brought back to the United States. He attests it is 99% copper and tin, which is consistent with antique Himalayan bowls from that region.

Inacio (2004) and Nur (2011) provide evidence regarding bowl types, physical shapes, and location of striking with puja in relation to waveguide synthesis. Inacio (2004) utilized waveguide synthesis technique for performing numerical simulations after bowls are played. His researchers used an experimental modal identification of three different Tibetan bowls then developed a systematic modeling approach. Extensive nonlinear numerical simulations were performed, for both impacted and rubbed bowls and the results are in good agreement with his preliminary experiments (Inacio, 2004). The numerical simulations shed light on the sound-producing mechanisms of Tibetan singing bowls. Both impact and friction excitations were addressed, including perfectly symmetrical and less than perfect bowls (a common occurrence).

The Dynamics of the puja (striking instrument) were also explored (Inacio 2004, Nur 2011). Excitation of HSB can include impact with the puja (striking like a bell), rubbing around the rim of the bowl or a combination of both. Both confirm rubbing the bowl results in less discord. Imperfect bowls such as the handmade HSB used in this experiment have more of a beat when rubbed versus the perfectly symmetrical machine made bowls.

Inacio's (2004), studies further revealed when the bowl is rubbed by the puja, a steady motion is never reached, for the bowl is disrupted whenever the vibration amplitude reaches a certain level. This motion results in severe "chaotic impacting," which breaks the mechanism of energy transfer, leading to a sudden decrease of amplitude. These findings had implications for this study and were incorporated into the development of how the HSB would be played during the research session. The researcher is attempting to achieve a relaxation response with study participants therefore the bowl must not be overplayed. When this occurs, the *singing* is converted to *ringing* and results in a displeasing chaotic chattering sound. This sonorous saturation effect, which can be musically interesting, is more like discord and contrary to the study goals.

Comparison studies by Inacio (2004) test a naked wood puja against one wrapped in soft cotton, which is then covered in leather. The naked puja, resulted in the initial transient becoming longer, before instability of the second mode (3.0) settled. The bowl responses were less regular, however six beats per revolution were clearly perceived. The results stress the importance of the contact/friction parameters, therefore if one wishes a bowl to "sing" in different modes this is easier to obtain in larger bowls. For the listener, sounds will always be perceived with a beating phenomena. However, for a perfectly symmetrical bowl, no beating is generated at the moving excitation point. For these reasons, a six-inch diameter handmade/imperfect metal Himalayan singing bowl was chosen for this research study, offering more beats when rubbed. A puja wrapped in soft cotton covered in leather on one end will be used to offer the purest bowl singing, with less incidence of the chattering sound.

Rationale for Directed Relaxation and Singing Bowl Pairing

This researcher was interested in studying the effects of adding the sound and vibration of HSB to a directed relaxation practice. In order to accomplish this goal, a combination of both Western and Eastern philosophies was considered. A thorough review of previous research conducted by the scientific community linking meditation to healing was analyzed. Then Eastern world research demonstrating sound, vibration and the relationship to healing was examined. The decision to create a directed relaxation for this study, as opposed to using TM approach was based on a few reasons. Although there is credible research proving the benefits of a specific transcendental meditation approach, the disadvantages of choosing TM include practicality and cost for most providers. TM technique requires weeks of sessions with a cost of $1500.00 (TM.org/ tuition). This researcher opted to offer a simple, affordable, user friendly, effective program for inducing relaxation. See Appendix A for the partial twenty-minute directed relaxation script developed and copyrighted. This is available to providers and laypersons requiring no advanced preparation, special skills or fees. Himalayan singing bowls vary in price ranging from $25.00 to thousands of dollars depending on size, composition and tone. The bowl used for this research project cost $150.00 and purchased at Circles of Wisdom in Andover, MA. The goal is to offer providers and laypersons a new, cost effective health improvement option while contributing to best practices for relaxation enhancement.

Overview of Related Research

Bridging the gap between the works of Seashore (1937) and Goldman (2008), Smith and Joyce (2004) investigated the relaxation states of students who listened to Mozart versus New Age Music. Researchers conducted a study with sixty-three students. Fourteen listened to a twenty-eight minute tape recording of Mozart's Eine Kleine Nachtmusik, fourteen listened to a twenty-eight minute tape of Steven Halpern's New Age Serenity Suite, and the remaining thirty-five chose magazines versus music. The time exposure was three consecutive days for twenty-eight minutes a session. Smith's (2001) fifteen relaxation state (R-State) categories were used as a measuring tool and included: sleepiness, disengagement, rested/refreshed, energized, physical relaxation, at ease/peace, joy, mental quiet, childlike innocence, thankfulness and love, mystery, awe and wonder, prayerfulness, and timeless/boundless/infinite, and awareness. Although no differences were noted after the first session, results indicated at the second session, participants who listened to Mozart reported higher levels of at ease/peace and lower levels of negative emotion. With session three the Mozart listeners reported substantially higher levels of mental quiet, awe and wonder, and mystery. Mozart listeners reported higher levels and New Age listeners slightly elevated levels of at ease/peace and rested/refreshed. Both groups reported higher levels of thankfulness and love compared to the magazine reading group.

Smith (2008) conducted a study to determine the effects of music on individuals suffering from anxiety. The efficacy of a music relaxation session was assessed using a group of adults working in a stressful consumer complaint call center in Queensdale. The employees were on the receiving end of angry customers and also subjected to verbal aggression from dissatisfied co-workers in the highly stressful environment. The stressor-strain framework, along with the Selye (1982) adaptation response was used to study eighty customer service specialists (female = 40, male = 40). The *state* portion of the State Trait Anxiety Inventory was used as a pre and post measurement. Results indicated the music relaxation intervention significantly reduced anxiety levels in participants compared to the group offered a discussion intervention. The music relaxation group exhibited a positive increase in feelings of relaxation and pleasantness, and decreased tension after the music relaxation intervention.

HSB Efficacy in Practice

Although there are a few field experts using HSB in practice (Gaynor, 1999; Nur 2011), a thorough search of literature represents a paucity of empirical data exploring the effects of the HSB on physiology. Dr. Mitchell Gaynor (1999), a traditional Western trained M.D. shares his first experience with a Tibetan singing bowl in his book *The Healing Power of Sound:*

"I began searching for healing modalities that could tangibly and reliably help my patients achieve these transformations. A turning point in my research occurred when I met Odsal who took me to a store where I picked out a Tibetan singing bowl. The exposure to the sound was so thrilling I began playing it every morning as part of my meditation practice. In a short time, I was less vulnerable to stress than I had been in the past. I could more easily avoid conflicts, as well as minor irritations that once would have made me lose my temper"(p. 11).

Limitations

It is important to understand that tones appealing to some may not be pleasing to others, depending on size, type, shape and sound. Therefore, the choice to use a handmade medium sized (six-inch) metal Himalayan singing bowl, may have affected participant responses. When struck, the bowl offers a deep resonance along with superb vibrational quality with a sustainable B^b ring tone. The particular bowl chosen for the study was based on tone and relaxing effects for this researcher.

Amplitude and decibel level are variables to consider, once the bowl is struck. Decibel (dB), named after Alexander Graham Bell (Martin, 1924) measures amplitude or loudness (intensity of sound). The bowl was played and struck at 70 dB, which is equivalent to normal conversation on the decibel scale. It falls in between department store (60 dB) and a vacuum cleaner (75 dB). The decibel level of the chosen bowl may not be comfortable to all participants.

Another potential limitation could be the size (six-inch diameter) with the specific B^b tone chosen for this study. Although pleasing to the researcher, it may not be pleasing to all study participants. Along the same lines as size and tone, *how* the bowl will be played may also be a limitation. Immediately before the DR session, the investigator will alternate striking the bowl until sound trail off (approximately thirty seconds for the first minute) then rubbing with the puja (second minute) for a total of twelve minutes. The researcher created this method, which includes sound trail off. By allowing the sound to come to a near stop, important space is created and believed to be necessary for healing. "It's the space where the transformational work of frequency shifting happens and change occurs—a powerful and sacred place that should be acknowledged and honored" (Goldman, 2008 p. 74). Deepak Chopra (1990) makes reference to the "fourth" state of consciousness, which exists beyond waking, sleeping or dreaming. In his book *Quantum Healing*, this state is described as, "absolute inner silence, a feeling of vast expansion, and a profound knowingness" (p.176). Based on Goldman and Chopra's work, this researcher built in the sacred space between intervals, when playing the HSB. Silence, may not be experienced by all participants equally.

Decisions on how to play the bowl (including length of time), were made after personal consultation, demonstration and instruction with Dr. Mitch Nur (2001). Nur has been involved with Eastern cultures for over thirty years, in specific areas of spiritual discipline, sacred sound practices, and healing techniques. Many, consider him a Master of Himalayan singing bowls. Having lived and studied in the Himalayas, he currently lectures and teaches various types of workshops throughout the United States on diverse world traditions involving sacred sound instruments. Although twelve minutes was a recommended time frame for the purpose of this project, this could have been a limitation and a longer time frame may have been needed by some participants to induce the relaxation effects desired.

The Chakras: Energy Centers and Bowl Tones

An intrinsic part of Hindu, Sufi and other Eastern philosophies include an understanding about the seven major energy centers located within the spinal column. These centers have influence on health and well-being of the whole body (Shapiro, 2006). Known as chakras, each one rises from a specific location and they work together with vibrations and energy flowing between them. Shapiro (2006) discusses how chakras influence the physical, mental and spiritual well-being in her book, *Your Body Speaks Your Mind*.

The first chakra, also known as the root, located in the perineum is associated with survival, trust, security and self-protection. Shapiro (2006) claims that weaknesses in this chakra create digestive and bowel problems linked to our stress response involving kidneys and adrenal glands. The second chakra, at the spine base called the sacral, is linked to desire, sexuality and reproduction. An undeveloped sacral chakra is responsible for exhaustion, decreased appetite, low sexual desire, lower back pain, menstrual and elimination issues. The third chakra, called the solar plexus, located behind the naval holds our personal power. When underdeveloped, fears, trust and responsibility issues are present. The fourth chakra, the heart, is located at the center of the chest and allows one to love and be loved. Problems with this chakra, manifest in breathing issues, such as asthma, along with heart, circulatory and breast illnesses. The fifth chakra, the throat, is located in the neck and houses communication and nourishment functions. Weaknesses can manifest in food and alcohol addictions. The sixth chakra, or third eye, is located in the forehead above the eyebrow center and holds perception, intuition and insight. A closed third eye chakra results in lack of awareness and gives rise to brain disorders including headaches, eyesight and hearing deficits. The final chakra, the crown, located at the top of the head is known as the *ultimate human experience* and is responsible for spiritual growth and cosmic consciousness. Weaknesses in the seventh chakra are connected to a loss of purpose, meaning and direction and can result in depressive illnesses (Shapiro, 2006).

The Chakras and Associated Note Scale

Kelly (2003) outlines the associations between the Chakras and corresponding musical note scale:

Chakras	Note	Vowel Sound
Root	C	UH
Sacral	D	OOO
Solar Plexus	E	OH
Heart	F	AH
Throat	G	EYE
Third Eye	A	AYE
Crown	B	EEE

To control for variables that could affect the study, it was important to determine the pitch of the bowl used, and match to it's corresponding chakra. The ring tone of the HSB used for this study was determined to be vibrating around a B^b pitch. Musician John Berman, used a Peterson strobe tuner, to make the determination when the bowl was struck with the leather covered end of the puja. Since the B note corresponds to the seventh, or crown chakra, individuals experiencing concerns with spiritual growth, meaning, purpose and direction, or those suffering from depressive illnesses may resonate more or less with this bowl. Since these variables will not be specifically addressed, it is included as a limitation.

Evaluation of Viable Research Designs

The study determined the physiological and relaxation effects of HSB exposure prior to a directed relaxation session using a quantitative correlational design. This design strategy was chosen to best answer the research questions proposed. Does adding HSB (potential stress reduction tool) prior to a meditation session have an effect on one's physiology? This experiment gathered pre and post session quantifiable data from fifty-one participants using physiological measurements (blood pressure and heart rate) at three intervals per session. Supplemental qualitative data was obtained twice per session by researcher, using Positive and Negative Rating Scale (PANAS). The two sessions were within two weeks and offered data from 102, fifty-minute sessions yielding 306 mean blood pressure and pulse readings along with 204 PANAS scores.

In light of this topic, similar studies were successful in measuring physiological relaxation effects using the quantitative design by Orme-Johnson and Walton (1998), Davidson et al. (2003), Schneider et al. (2005), Bjerklie et al. (2003), and Benson (1975). The major strength of this approach is the adequate sample size. Conclusions can be drawn based on the results obtained from the questions proposed. The quantitative design is in alignment with the purpose of the proposed study and the research questions outlined. A mixed method or qualitative approach would not be possible or practical based on questions proposed.

Chapter 2 Summary

Based on the number of studies previously cited, it is clear that incorporating various relaxation techniques such as TM, singing, meditation, and sound exposure proves physical and emotional health benefits. In the absence of empirical data demonstrating the efficacy of HSB exposure on DR practice, this project attempted to show a correlation between enhanced physiology and HSB exposure prior to DR practice. Results will add to the current body of knowledge regarding the impact of sound and vibration on physiology. This study is unique. A review of literature indicates that previous research has not yet examined whether or not there is a relationship between lower blood pressure, heart rate, and an increase in positive effects after exposure to HSB session prior to directed relaxation compared to a silence session. Results from this research project will add a new dimension to the body of literature exploring complementary methods to enhance the relaxation response.

CHAPTER 3

METHODOLOGY

Introduction

Building on prior research, health care providers are challenged to discover and implement innovative methods that could enhance the relaxation response aiding in stress management including anxiety and depressive symptoms thereby promoting improved mental and physical well-being. Dr. Herbert Benson (1975), one of the first medical doctors to discover the *relaxation response* was able to objectively measure the relationship between stressful psychological events and the associated physiological changes affecting one's health.

Over the decades since Benson's work, complementary and alternative methods CAM have emerged to help manage stress. Individuals practicing Eastern CAM make claims that exposure to the sound and vibration of the HSB induce deeper relaxation effects on the mind and body due to its unique resonance (Adero, 2001; Goldman, 2008). Specifically, Himalayan singing bowls HSB have been used for ceremonial and meditation purposes, and are being used by practitioners to enhance relaxation and meditation (Huyser, 1999). The specific physiological effects of HSB have not been measured. The intent of this research project was to determine differences between HSB exposure prior to a directed relaxation DR session and one without HSB exposure (silence session).

Researcher's Philosophy

Results from this study will make a significant contribution to the scientific body of knowledge in the relaxation response field. Based on outcomes from this study, clinicians will have the option of including HSB session prior to a meditation session when attempting to enhance the relaxation response. HSB inclusion enhances positive physiology aiding in stress management. This effect, based on prior studies (Benson, 1975; Bjerklie et al., 2003) will improve both physical and mental well-being leading to a greater quality of life. This project will encourage additional studies in the area of how sound and vibration could impact relaxation and stress management.

This researcher, a practitioner in private practice, is intrigued by the concept of combining Eastern and Western traditions when working with clients exhibiting a number of stress-related disorders. This project attempted to measure the physiological and psychological effects of adding HSB prior to a meditation practice. The purpose of this chapter includes identifying the methodology utilized (quantitative method) and specific research design implemented. The study was designed to determine the physiological (blood pressure and heart rate) along with psychological effects (PANAS) when adding a twelve-minute HSB exposure prior to a twenty-minute meditation practice compared to the same session with silence. Permission to use PANAS was obtained from Dr. David Watson, author of the tool.

A quantitative correlational design was used to answer the research questions proposed as a means to enhance best practices in the field of meditation by determining if adding HSB (potential stress reduction tool) prior to a meditation session has an effect on one's physiological reactions (outcome measures) including blood pressure, heart rate and overall feeling of relaxation.

In my psychotherapeutic work with clients in distress, I use a combination of Eastern and Western techniques to promote wellness, namely; breath work and directed relaxation DR to promote the relaxation response. There are a number of mental health and alternative medicine practitioners who make claims that hearing the sound and feeling the vibration of someone playing a Himalayan singing bowl HSB promotes a greater sense of relaxation and well-being. A review of the literature yields no specific empirical studies proving the cardiovascular and mental health effects of this practice. The purpose of this project was to explore the effects of HSB exposure prior to a twenty-minute directed relaxation DR session. This experiment gathered quantifiable data from physiological measurements (systolic/diastolic blood pressure and heart rate) along with supplemental qualitative data taken from researcher administered and participant rated PANAS scale assessing positive and negative affect scores pre and post sessions.

Research Design

The study determined physiological responses along with positive and negative affect changes comparing a twelve-minute HSB exposure to the same time period using silence prior to a twenty-minute directed relaxation session. The researcher proposed a quantitative correlational design to answer research questions with the hypothesis: there is a positive relationship between the use of HSB including enhanced relaxation and positive physiological effects when used prior to DR. There was a desire to explore possible differences in affect states and physiology comparing HSB to silence when offered prior to a pre-recorded twenty-minute directed relaxation session. This experiment gathered pre and post session quantifiable data from physiological measurements (blood pressure and heart rate) and supplemental qualitative data taken from researcher administered Positive and Negative Rating Scale (PANAS).

Research Design Strategy

The study included a sample size of fifty-one adult males and females and determined the physiological and relaxation effects of HSB exposure prior to a directed relaxation session versus a silence session. The researcher utilized a quantitative correlational design to answer research questions proposed.

Research Questions and Hypothesis

The primary research question (1) and sub questions (2-3) in this study:

1. What are the physiological and relaxation effects when integrating HSB exposure prior to directed relaxation (DR) session?
2. Will the HSB produce an enhanced effect on blood pressure and heart rate when added prior to DR session versus no HSB exposure prior to a meditation session?

3. Will there be an enhanced relaxation experience measuring positive and negative affect (PANAS rating scale) with HSB exposure prior to a directed relaxation session as opposed to no HSB exposure prior to directed relaxation session?

Directional Hypothesis

Directional Hypothesis: There is a positive relationship between the use of HSB and enhanced relaxation and positive physiological effects when used prior to DR. Does adding HSB (potential stress reduction tool) prior to a meditation session have an effect on one's physiology? This experiment gathered pre, middle, and post session quantifiable data from physiological measurements (blood pressure and heart rate) and supplemental qualitative data taken from researcher administered Positive and Negative Rating Scale (PANAS). This credible research design offered results useful to both Western and Eastern practice fields. This quantitative method was chosen based on the research questions and field of inquiry being studied. The experiment was based on defined variables measured within a finite time period to establish cause and effect. The independent variable is the HSB. The dependent variable is the meditation session.

Sampling Design and Setting

Participants were drawn from a fifty-mile radius in an affluent suburb located twenty miles northeast of Boston, Massachusetts. The town includes the researcher's private practice where a great majority of clients are being treated for anxiety and depression. Stress management is an important component of most client interventions. Drawing research results from this demographic will aid the researcher by enhancing best practices for relaxation and stress management in a suburb closely connected to a major United States city.

The town, in Essex County, Massachusetts, United States, was incorporated in 1646, and as of 2010 census, the population was 33,201. It is part of the Boston-Cambridge-Quincy, Massachusetts and New Hampshire metropolitan statistical area. The population includes a mixture of working class, suburban elite and lower income with a majority holding a bachelor's, associate or graduate degree. Of the total population there are 1,111 more females to males. The majority of the population is 40-64 years old: 96.13% are white and native born in the state. The majority of homes are owner-occupied. The median household income is $60,040 compared to the national average of $44, 512 (Zillow, 2010).

Fifty-six adult male and female participants (age eighteen or older with no age cap) were recruited from a fifty-mile radius of the town chosen in Massachusetts. To determine adequacy of sample size, prior research projects measuring blood pressure were reviewed. Conlin (2008) and Vollmer (2005), using forty-two participants, demonstrated changes in blood pressure with a SD of 9.7 mm Hg for systolic and 7.9 mm Hg for diastolic using non-pharmacologic interventions. A total of forty-two participants in the crossover study had 90% power to detect a difference at a two-sided 0.05 significance level of 5 mm Hg for systolic blood pressure and 4 mm Hg for diastolic blood pressure.

Although many people benefit from the relaxation response, Lazarus (1990) makes the argument that some appear "allergic" and for that population, relaxation offerings should be approached with caution. This researcher attempted to avoid causing harm by screening participants during phone interview for past negative relaxation experiences. Knowledge of the allergic potential facilitated the availability of proper interventions, should problems occur during the study.

Caution would be used for participants with a history of anxiety disorder in an effort to avoid relaxation-induced anxiety (Heide & Borkovec, 1984). Individuals with asthma, represent another potential at risk population. According to Lehrer et al. (1986) relaxation tends to decrease sympathetic activity or reactivity, and individuals with small-airway obstruction may experience a counter-therapeutic effect if they have airway dilation in response to sympathetic autonomic nervous system stimulation.

With the above considerations in mind, a management strategy suggested by Lazarus (1984) was incorporated into the directed relaxation script. Positive or pleasant imagery is often helpful (Lazarus, 1984) if the subject exhibits unpleasant side effects of the relaxation. Focusing on the guided imagery of *clear blue sky* was repeated multiple times during the DR. The room was intentionally kept well-lighted in an effort to minimize fear (Lazarus, 1984). Furthermore, all subjects were asked to remain seated rather than laying down thus creating a greater feeling of being in control. The researcher's voice tone remained calm, slow and focused on the pre-recorded directed relaxation throughout both sessions.

Participants had blood pressure and heart rate readings automatically tracked during the entire session. If there were signs of counter relaxation as described above, the session would have been stopped immediately. The researcher, trained in CPR and advanced life support, would have provided on-site intervention. If advanced emergency medical technician response was needed, the local police and fire station was located less than a half mile from the research location. None of the participants had asthma, or experienced an adverse effect from the sessions.

Informed Consent

All participants provided written informed consent after receiving an explanation of the voluntary nature of their participation and a description of the study. This single researcher conducted all sessions with fifty-six individuals required to return for a second session within two weeks of the first. Informed consent included; why they were being asked to participate, how many would be in the study, who was paying for the study, fees required, length of time required (2) fifty-minute sessions in the same office within two weeks of each other, and the study location. See appendix for full informed consent form. If the participant decided to be in this study and if they signed the consent form, they were expected to do the following:

- Give personal information about themselves, such as age and gender.
- Answer questions during an interview about how relaxed they feel.
- Complete a survey about positive and negative emotional states.
- Allow the researcher to observe them as they relax during a pre-recorded directed meditation session.
- Allow the researcher to look at their data collected during the sessions.

While they were in the study, they were expected to:

- Follow the instructions given.
- Tell the researcher if they wanted to stop being in the study at any time.

The participants were informed the researcher would not be audio or videotaping any sessions. Potential risks and possible discomfort were explained. The signed consent indicated their permission to have an automatic blood pressure (BP) cuff applied to their arm to monitor heart rate and (BP) throughout the fifty-minute sessions.

It was explained this is similar to what they may have experienced in their doctor's office. A sensation of slight tightness may occur when the cuff is inflating for the series of readings taken during the two sessions. They understood the right to change their mind about being in the study and at any time they could choose to stop without penalty. Participants did not receive any compensation for being in the fully voluntary study.

The researcher could have them removed from the study at any time if:

- The researcher believed it was best for them to stop being in the study.
- They did not follow directions about the study.
- They no longer met inclusion criteria required to participate.

They were informed that all personal information was kept confidential such as name, age etc. Data was collected with pen and paper on site at researcher's private practice office, which remained secure. To ensure confidentiality, the participants were identified by number rather than by name. Only the researcher and academic supervisor were able to view the information gathered. All results and materials collected remained confidential and stored in a password-protected computer. In any written reports or publications, no one would be able to identify the study participants.

In general, the researcher can assure participants' confidentiality. There may be times when this is not possible if:

- The researcher finds out a child or vulnerable adult has been abused.
- The researcher finds out a person plans to harm him or herself.
- The researcher finds out that a person plans to harm someone else.

The above are based on laws in this state requiring mental health professionals to take action if they think a person might harm themselves or another, or if a child or adult is being abused. In addition, there are guidelines researchers must follow to ensure all people are treated with respect and kept safe.

The participant was encouraged to ask questions about this issue before agreeing to be in the study, since it is important participants do not feel betrayed if the researcher is required to breach confidentiality. Participants were encouraged to ask questions about all other aspects of the study at any time, and were offered the researcher's private cell number if they had further concerns, complaints, or became ill. Informed consent includes the University's Research Integrity

Office (RIO) number, established to protect the rights and welfare of human research participants.

RIO could be contacted for any of the following reasons:

- They have questions about rights as a research participant.
- They wish to discuss problems or concerns.
- They have suggestions to improve the participant experience.
- They do not feel comfortable talking with the researcher.

They were instructed the RIO can be contacted at any time. Confidentiality would be maintained unless there was a concern involving the safety of an individual.

Sampling Procedures

The research experiment initially started with a sample size of fifty-six adult male and female participants located in a suburban community within a fifty-mile radius of Boston, MA. Whenever large numbers of participants are needed, a convenience sample is justified (Creswell, 2009). The design was created to compare the two conditions, with no random assignment. In an effort to minimize variables, the individuals served as their own control. Convenience sampling was used with flyers posted in local downtown public places including the library, medical offices, senior center, bookstores and market within a fifteen-mile radius of the research location. There were no conflict of interest issues between the researcher and flyer locations, which advertised two free relaxation sessions over a two-week period of time with a trained licensed psychotherapist.

Interested participants were instructed to call the number on the flyer connecting them directly to the researcher. Upon arrival participants produced their license to confirm age of consent. It was explained they would be attending two, fifty-minute sessions within two weeks of each other in an effort to assist the researcher's understanding of stress management and relaxation (see Appendix D). All participants were offered written informed consent after receiving an explanation of the voluntary nature of their participation and a description of the study. There was no payment or other form of compensation offered. Once they agreed, directions to the research location were provided and participants were scheduled for the sessions. Both sessions took place in the researcher's private office, which was posted on the flyer.

One might argue this strategy may result in a potentially biased sample, based on the fact they responded and agreed to participate. This is expected with a large recruitment effort. Even if a random method was chosen, the participants' decision to participate, or not, would in and of itself result in some bias.

Instruments and Measures

HSB Intervention – The bowl was played by the investigator for twelve minutes immediately before the DR session (time determined after discussion with Mitch Nur, Ph.D., personal communication, July 15, 2011). To control for as many variables as possible, it was important to determine the tone of this particular study bowl. When the six-inch HSB was struck using the leather covered puja, musician John Bermani used a Petersen Strobe Tuner to determine the B^b vibrational tone (see Appendix E).

Silence Intervention – On the non-bowl group session, the individual was asked to get comfortable and the researcher left the room for twelve minutes.

Measures

1. Blood pressure and heart rate: An automatic blood pressure cuff (device called IntelliSense manufactured by Omron, Model # HEM-747IC) was used to obtain and record preset interval data (blood pressure and heart rate) using numerical scores. Pre-session blood pressure and heart rates were taken and repeated after the twelve minutes of either silence or HSB intervention. Repeat measures were taken a third time after the twenty-minute DR.

2. Relaxation effect:

   A. The participant was asked if there were any new stressful events in their lives when they returned for the second session within two weeks of the first session. There were no events reported that would have eliminated participants from the study.

   B. Participants completed the Positive and Negative Affect Scale (PANAS) pre and post session. PANAS has been used to effectively measure positive and negative affect states in a number of research studies. Clinical improvements were evaluated using PANAS scores in patients with deep brain stimulation for treatment resistant depression (Mayberg et al., 2005). Positive and negative affect states were measured with PANAS along with associated mindfulness with rock climbers (Steinberg, 2011) and bungee jumpers (Middleton et al., 1996). Lord and Menz

(2002) used PANAS to assess mobility, physical functioning and overall cardiovascular fitness after incorporation of a six-minute walk program for older adults. Health-risk behavior in adolescents was correlated with increasing emotional response to music when PANAS was used in Robert et al.'s (1998) study. As in the proposed study, when there is a desire to accurately measure positive and negative affect states, the PANAS has been proven to be a valid and reliable tool.

The reliabilities of the PANAS scales, as measured by Cronbach's alpha, were .89 for PA and .85 for NA. The narrowness of the confidence limits associated with these coefficients indicate they can be regarded as providing very accurate estimates of the internal consistency of the PANAS in the general adult population. Thus, both PA and NA scale can be viewed as possessing adequate reliability (Crawford & Henry, 2004).

Construct validity, measurement properties and normative data using PANAS was administered to a non-clinical sample (N = 1,003) broadly representative of the general adult population in the United Kingdom (Crawford & Henry, 2004). Competing models of the latent structure PANAS were evaluated using confirmatory factor analysis. Correlational analysis and regression were used to determine the influence of demographic variables on the PANAS scores and relationship between the PANAS with measures of depression and anxiety (HADS and DASS). Results indicated the best-fitting model of the latent structure of PANAS consisted of two factors corresponding to positive affect and negative affect scales. This permitted correlated error between items drawn from the same mood subcategories (Zevon & Tellegen, 1982). Demographic variables had only very modest influences on PANAS scores and the PANAS exhibited measurement invariance across demographic subgroups. Reliability of PANAS was high, and the pattern of relationships between PANAS, DASS and HADS were consistent with tripartite theory (belief, truth, and justification). Crawford and Henry (2004) concluded PANAS is a reliable and valid measure of the constructs it was intended to assess. The utility of this measure is enhanced by the large-scale normative data.

Watson and Walker (1996) examined the long-term temporal stability and predictive validity of trait Positive Affect and Negative Affect scales. Participants were initially assessed as undergraduates, rating how they felt overall (general sample) or during the previous year (year sample). Retesting occurred on a general affect measure and on scales assessing current depression and anxiety approximately six years for the general sample or seven (year sample) later. All participants had graduated from college and most were employed full-time. Negative affect scores decreased significantly over the study period and the Negative and Positive Affect scales both displayed a significant and moderate level of stability. In addition, initial scores on both scales correlated significantly with measures of current symptoms completed several years later. Researchers concluded trait affect scales were substantially stable and maintained significant prediction power, even across extended time spans (Watson & Walker, 1996).

In follow-up to PANAS, a ten-item short form was developed and tested by Thompson (2007) for validity. These validation studies included a large sample size ($N = 1,789$), and researchers compared the original twenty-item PANAS which I am proposing for this study, to a newer ten-item short form

I-PANAS-SF. Thompson (2007) was able to confirm the cross-sample stability, internal reliability, temporal stability, cross-cultural factorial invariance, and convergent and criterion-related validities with the PANAS ten-item short form. Although all were found to be psychometrically acceptable (Thompson, 2007), this researcher chose the twenty-item original longer version PANAS since there are more studies confirming its validity and reliability (Crawford & Henry, 2004; Lord & Menz, 2002; Mayberg et al., 2005; Middleton et al., 1996; Roberts et al., 1998; Steinberg, 2011; Watson &Walker, 1996; Zevon & Tellegen, 1982).

Data Collection

In an effort to control variables that could affect the relaxation response, the study environment was the same community office setting used for all sessions. Since the individual served as their own control, they were required to return for the second session within two weeks. Blood pressure, heart rate and affect response ratings (PANAS) were measured prior to and after directed relaxation DR session with and without HSB exposure. To avoid the introduction of a fixed variable and an ordering effect, a coin toss was used to randomly assign singing bowl or silence intervention on the first session followed by receipt of the alternative at the second session. Before the second session, the client was asked if there were any significant events in their lives between the first and second session. It was the therapist's discretion to use the data from the session if client reported a significant event that could impact study results (traumatic event such as sudden death of loved one, motor vehicle accident) since first session. There were no incidents requiring study elimination.

The dependent measures of interest were blood pressure (BP), heart rate (HR) and PANAS. The mean of three readings (BP and HR) were recorded to reduce the variance seen with only a single reading, and were taken at the same time on three different intervals during both sessions (baseline, first (after intervention) and second measurement (final taken at end of session). PANAS scores were taken twice in both sessions at the beginning and the end. Changes in BP, HR and PANAS across sessions were calculated. Sessions with and without the bowl (experimental versus control), control days (silence) versus bowl days, were then compared using paired T-tests and repeated measures ANOVAS.

If randomly assigned to receive HSB first, the bowl was played by the investigator for twelve minutes immediately before DR session. Since sound trail off occurs around thirty seconds, the bowl was struck softly every thirty seconds. The bowl was played by the researcher sitting on the couch next to the participant creating a twelve-inch bowl distance from participant's right ear for the fifty-five participants, and was played into the opposite ear at the same distance for the mastectomy participant. All data was collected within a thirty-day period and all sessions took place in the same researcher's private practice office with participants sitting upright on the office couch. Blood pressure readings were obtained using the same cuff for all subjects who remained attached but un-inflated throughout both sessions. The cuff was applied to the left arm in fifty-five participants, and to the right in one, due to a history of having a mastectomy on the left side.

On the non-bowl group session, the individual was asked to get comfortable and the researcher left the room for twelve minutes. Blood pressure and pulse readings were obtained before session, after twelve minutes and at the end of session.

Participants completed the Positive and Negative Affect Scale (PANAS) pre and post session.

Data Analysis Procedures

The dependent measures of interest were blood pressure, heart rate and PANAS. All blood pressure and heart rate results represent the mean of three sets of readings for each time period. There are three mean blood pressure and heart rate readings for control session and bowl session (six scores). Statistical analyses were completed using SPSS (version XX, 2011, IBM Corporation). Two-way analysis of days was used to measure the differences between all variables on day one compared to all variables on day two with fifty-one subjects ($n = 102$). The data represents a two-way repeated measure analysis of variance on two factors using a balanced design. The general linear model analysis mode was used for repeated measures with the same person having multiple measures. ANCOVA allowed the researcher to analyze change from baseline while including age, sex and baseline measurements as covariates. Changes in outcome measures were accounted while controlling for the influence of the above parameters. These determined if response over time was significant when controlling for age, sex and baseline. The sample size in all analyses was fifty-one. PANAS scores were taken twice in both sessions. Changes in BP, heart rate and PANAS across sessions were calculated. Sessions with and without the bowl (experimental versus control), control days versus bowl days, were then compared using paired T-tests and repeated measures ANOVAS.

Limitations of Research Design

One limitation could have been drop-out rate after the first session. Fifty-six participants attended session one, and five were eliminated due to their inability to return for session two. Session one data sets from these five subjects were eliminated from the study. Other limitations could include the homogeneity of the group as well as the final sample size of fifty-one. Additional studies could include only clients with hypertension using a similar approach with specific age groups: (20-40, 41-60, 61-80) for comparison. Future research could be done utilizing crystal singing bowls versus metal, to determine similarities or result differences.

Internal Validity

When conducting credible research, it is imperative to control for extraneous variables. Conclusions can be drawn from the observed effects such as those solely attributed to HSB (treatment variable). To achieve this, the same person served as their own control, while being exposed to the same conditions. Paired T-testing was done using data from the same individual on two successive measures, comparing paired data sets to determine mean blood pressures and heart rates, taken in three intervals during the fifty-minute session. The researcher is confident that conclusions drawn are warranted from the data collected and methodology used.

External Validity

External validity refers to the extent to which study results will apply to situations beyond *this* study. By identifying and reporting a measureable relaxation response after HSB the results may be generalizable to particular meditation practices.

Expected Findings

1. There would be a statistically significant decrease in systolic BP across the course of each session.
2. It was expected systolic BP would decrease in both HSB session and non-HSB sessions, but the change during HSB will be greater versus non-HSB.
3. I did not expect pulse or diastolic BP to be affected within the time frame allotted for the experiment.
4. In both HSB and non-HSB, I expected significant increases in positive and significant decreases in negative affect scores. However, the change is expected to be significantly greater during HSB sessions.
5. All participants would experience a greater feeling of relaxation after both sessions.

Ethical Issues

Ethical considerations are woven into the research plan to ensure respect for participants and research sites. The Belmont Report, generated from the Department of Health, Education, and Welfare, on July 12, 1974, established the National Research Act (Pub. L. 93-348) and was signed into law. This created the National Commission for the Protection of Human Subjects of

Biomedical and Behavioral Research. A core tenet; informed consent ensures the respect for persons and requires subjects, to the degree they are capable, be given the opportunity to choose what shall or shall not happen to them (Belmont Report, 1979).

Another aspect to consider includes the presence of beneficence. Respect for persons ensures that the individuals being treated are autonomous agents, and persons with diminished autonomy are entitled to protection. This study will not include participants with diminished autonomy (minors and those with diminished mental health capacity). In addition, participants will be protected from harm. Respecting autonomy will include considering opinions and choices. This research study involving human subjects, took all measures needed to ensure the participants entered into the project voluntarily and with adequate information. Participants in this study were not put at risk and those who were vulnerable and needing protection (minors under age 18), were excluded from participating.

Participants signed informed consent explaining the study and they understand participation was voluntary. Informed consent included: identification of the researcher/sponsoring institution, how participants were selected, and research criteria designed to meet study goals. Additional items included: the purpose of the research, benefits of participating (complementary meditation session), level of participant involvement, possible risks (none anticipated), guarantee of confidentiality, assurance of withdrawal at any time, and provision of researcher's contact number for additional questions.

This single researcher conducted all sessions with fifty-six individuals who completed first session and fifty-one who returned for second session within two weeks. Data was collected with pen and paper on site at researcher's private practice office and remained secure. Participants were assigned a number to maintain anonymity. All materials related to research were sealed then transported to a totally secure location for tabulation. All results were stored in a password-protected computer and remained confidential. Only the researcher and academic supervisor were able to view information. In written reports or publications, all results and materials collected remained confidential.

Chapter 3 Summary

The researcher predicted there would be a significant change in the parasympathetic nervous system as measured by blood pressure and heart rate along with a heightened relaxation response, as indicated by PANAS scores after adding HSB prior to the twenty-minute DR. Findings were expected to indicate it is worthwhile to consider the role of a twelve-minute exposure to HSB prior to a twenty-minute directed relaxation session for enhanced physiological and psychological effects. The quantitative method chosen, and choice of data collection and analysis, clearly aligns with the research problem and questions outlined. The primary research question (1) and sub questions (2-3) the proposed study will address:

1. What are the physiological and relaxation effects when integrating HSB exposure prior to a directed relaxation DR session?

    Results for the first question addressing the physiological effects were evident in pre and post blood pressure and heart rate readings. These were compared with the second session to determine statistically significant differences between session with and without HSB exposure. The researcher expected to see a statistically significant decrease in systolic blood pressure across the course of each session. It may follow, if systolic BP is significantly decreased in both HSB session and non HSB sessions, the change during HSB will be greater versus non HSB. Systolic blood pressure is more susceptible to changes associated with short-term external circumstances. Heart rate, similar to diastolic pressure is not usually influenced with a short-term relaxation intervention (Paul R. Conlin, MD, personal communication, October 29, 2011).

In the HSB session, the researcher expected significant increases in positive affect scores (interested, excited, strong, enthusiastic, proud, alert, inspired, determined, attentive and active), and decreases in negative affect scores (distressed, upset, guilty, scared, hostile, irritable, ashamed, nervous, jittery and afraid). Results of this study will add scientific evidence to the claims (Adero, 2001; Goldman, 2008; Nur, 2011) that exposure to the sound and vibration of HSB induces deeper relaxation effects on the mind and body due to its unique resonance.

2. Will HSB produce an enhanced effect on blood pressure and heart rate when added prior to DR session versus no HSB exposure prior to a meditation session?

3. Will there be an enhanced relaxation experience (PANAS) with HSB exposure prior to a meditation session as opposed to no HSB exposure prior to mediation session?

CHAPTER 4

DATA ANALYSIS AND RESULTS

Introduction

This study was designed to determine the physiological and psychological effects of adding exposure to Himalayan singing bowl HSB prior to directed relaxation DR session. Chapter Four offers a non-evaluative reporting of the data collected in the study. Findings will be supported, using tables and graphs to help illustrate study results.

The directional hypothesis guiding the study and the research questions:

There is a positive relationship between exposure to HSB and physiological and relaxation responses when used prior to DR.

The primary research question (1) and sub questions (2-3) in the completed study are:

1. What are the physiological and relaxation effects of integrating exposure to HSB prior to DR session?

2. Will HSB produce an enhanced effect on blood pressure and heart rate when added prior to DR session compared to no HSB exposure?

3. Will there be an enhanced relaxation experience, as measured by positive and negative affect (PANAS) with HSB exposure prior to DR session compared to no HSB exposure?

Description of the Sample

In this study, a convenience sampling was utilized by recruiting adult participants through flyers posted in public places (e.g. library, medical offices, senior center, book stores and market) within a fifteen-mile radius of the research location in Massachusetts. This suburban community is located twenty miles northeast of Boston, Massachusetts. Fifty-six adult male and female participants were recruited. All reported to the first session, where informed consent was obtained, and each participant enrolled in the study. The design was created to compare the two conditions with no random assignment, for the individual was required to return for the second session within a week thus serving as their own control minimizing study variables. Five of the initial participants were unable to return for second session within the allotted time frame therefore, data from those participants was removed resulting in fifty-one participants completing both, totaling one hundred and two sessions. There were sixteen males and thirty-five females ranging in age from twenty-six to sixty-nine with a mean age of 50.52. This sample is representative of the town's majority population, 40-64 years old.

The adequacy of sample size is based on studies measuring change in systolic and diastolic blood pressure in response to non-pharmacologic interventions (Conlin, 2008 & Vollmer, 2005), where repeated measurements of blood pressure in individuals with normal and high blood pressure generated a Standard Deviation (SD) of 9.7 mm Hg for systolic blood pressure and 7.9 mm Hg for diastolic blood pressure. Thus, forty-two participants in a crossover study had 90% power to detect a difference of 5 mm Hg for systolic blood pressure and 4 mm Hg for diastolic blood pressure at a two-sided 0.05 significance level.

Summary of Results

The findings in this study supported the directional hypothesis affirming there was a positive effect from HSB exposure prior to directed relaxation DR on physiological responses. Blood pressure and heart rate fell significantly over time in both the HSB and silence groups. There was a statistically significant difference in the change in systolic and diastolic blood pressure over time with the HSB group having a greater decline when compared to the silence group. Heart rate fell in a similar pattern to blood pressures. Participants who were hypertensive at baseline had the same qualitative responses but when compared to the normotensives, the hypertensives had a statistically significant difference in their response to the bowl session.

Positive and negative affect scores on PANAS revealed a similar response in both the bowl and the silence sessions. Both scores fell significantly, with no statistically significant difference between the two sessions. Analysis of ten individual sub-scores for both the positive and negative composites indicated all fell in parallel with the total scores. Results revealed a consistent drop in both positive and negative due to the relaxation response elicited using twenty-minute directed relaxation regardless of bowl versus silence preceding the session.

Details of Analysis and Results

The directional hypothesis along with the research questions guided the study. I hypothesized a positive relationship between the use of HSB exposure and enhanced relaxation and positive physiological effects when used prior to directed relaxation DR. The primary research question (1) and sub questions (2–3) were:

1. What are the physiological and relaxation effects of integrating exposure to HSB prior to DR session?
2. Will the HSB produce an enhanced effect on blood pressure and pulse rate when added prior to DR session when compared to no HSB exposure?
3. Will there be an enhanced relaxation experience as measured by positive and negative affect (PANAS) with HSB exposure prior to DR session when compared to no HSB exposure?

SPSS was used to obtain the two-way analysis of days measuring differences between all variables on one day compared to all variables on the return day with fifty-one subjects. Measures are illustrated in the Table below with mean values (± SD) shown. In all analyses N the sample size was fifty-one and all blood pressure and heart rate results represent the mean of three sets of readings for each time period (baseline, first and second). The twenty-minute directed relaxation was a constant and followed both intervention groups just prior to the second readings.

Using descriptive statistics, the mean systolic has a greater decrease in the bowl group comparing baseline HSB (132.2) second measurement HSB (122.5) compared to silence baseline (133.9) to second measurement silence (127.1) with standard deviation showing even disbursement across all sets. The mean diastolic measurement reveals a greater drop in diastolic with bowl group baseline at 81.2 to 79.2 at second measurement compared to the same reading for silence (83.5 and ending at 83.2). Heart rate changes indicate a deeper drop in the bowl group, comparing baseline (75) to second (68.7) versus silence (72.8) to second (69.5). Positive PANAS scores resulted in both groups falling significantly but indicating no difference between the baseline and final positive PANAS baseline and positive PANAS second in bowl (34.0 to 30.5) versus silence (34.0 to 31.2) groups. Negative PANAS scores indicated both groups falling significantly having greater decreases in the bowl group. Although there was no statistically significant difference between the baseline and final negative PANAS in bowl (13.8 to 10.8) versus silence groups (12.7 to 10.4), the bowl group had greater decreases in negative scores.

Table 1 illustrates the mean systolic and diastolic blood pressure, which fell significantly in both groups over time ($p < 0.001$). While the HSB group had greater declines, there was no significant intervention x time interaction. Heart rate fell significantly in both groups ($p < 0.05$) and there was a significant intervention x time interaction ($p = 0.004$), with heart rate significantly lower in the HSB group. Both positive PANAS and negative PANAS scores fell significantly in both groups over time ($p < 0.001$). Although there was a greater decline in the HSB group there was no significant intervention x time interaction.

Table 1.

Mean Systolic and Diastolic Blood Pressure

Time Period	Intervention	SBP (mm Hg)	DBP (mm Hg)	HR (per min)	PANAS Positive	PANAS Negative
Baseline	HSB	132.2 (19.1)	81.2 (11.0)	75.0 (11.5)	34.0 (7.8)	13.8 (5.0)
	Silence	133.9 (18.2)	83.5 (11.1)	72.8 (10.6)	34.0 (7.1)	12.7 (3.6)
First Measurement	HSB	124.2 (16.2)	78.6 (10.2)	71.4 (10.5)		
	Silence	125.9 (18.1)	80.7 (10.9)	69.5 (9.3)		
Second Measurement	HSB	122.5 (17.4)	79.2 (9.8)	68.7 (9.3)	30.5 (10.2)	10.8 (1.8)
	Silence	127.1 (17.6)	83.2 (11.6)	69.5 (9.0)	31.2 (8.8)	10.4 (1.2)

Note. Values are mean (SD); SBP = systolic blood pressure; DBP = diastolic blood pressure; HR = heart rate

Change in Parameters Over Time

The previous analyses looked at each BP and heart rate measurement separately (baseline, first, and second). The ANCOVA allows the researcher to analyze change in BP and HR from baseline including age, sex and baseline measurements as covariates. This enables the researcher to adjust the changes for these parameters. With the prior three sets of measures (pre, post and post2), we now have subtracted post from pre, which now represents delta 1, and subtracting post2 from pre, we have delta 2. ANCOVA will assist in determining if you control for age and sex, will baseline change over time.

Delta systolic blood pressure by age and gender results indicate a greater difference between the bowl group from time 1 = 8.0 to time 2 = 9.6 compared to silence group time 1 = 7.8 to time 2 = 6.8. Delta diastolic blood pressure results indicate a decrease in bowl group 1 = 2.6 to time 2 = 2.0 compared to silence group time 1 = 2.8 to time 2 = 0.34. Heart rate results indicate statistically significant difference in bowl group from time 1= 3.6 to time 2 = 6.3 compared to silence group time 1= 3.3 to time 2 = 3.2. The changes in systolic blood pressure and heart rate were significantly different with the HSB intervention compared to silence intervention with significant time x intervention interaction ($p = 0.044$ and $p = 0.003$, respectively). The change in diastolic blood pressure was greater in the HSB group with a non- significant trend ($p = 0.073$).

Figures 1-3 plot the mean change in systolic and diastolic blood pressure and heart rate. In each case, the HSB intervention had a more sustained effect versus silence intervention. Table 2 provides the descriptive statistics for the interventions.

Figure 1: Change in Systolic Blood Pressure

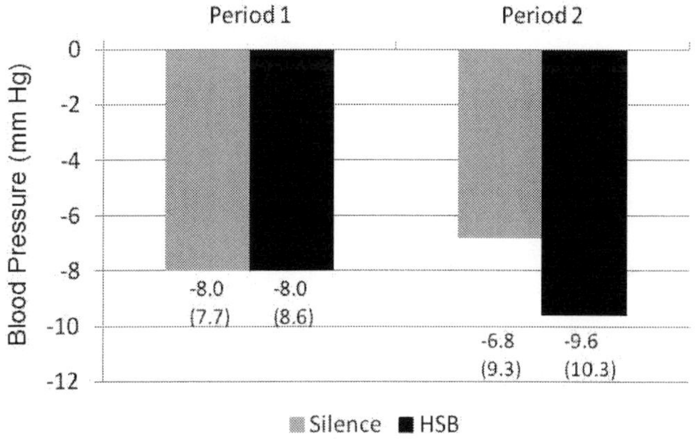

Mean (SD)
ANCOVA adjusting for baseline, age, sex
P=0.044 Silence vs. Bowl

Jayan Marie Landry PhD

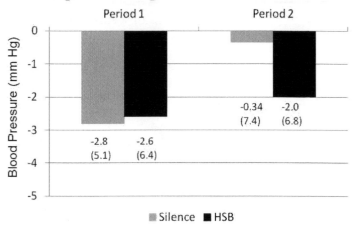

Figure 2: Change in Diastolic Blood Pressure

Mean (SD)
ANCOVA adjusting for baseline, age, sex
P=0.073 Silence vs. Bowl

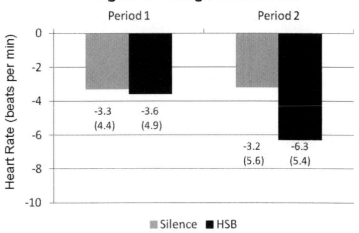

Figure 3: Change in Heart Rate

Mean (SD)
ANCOVA adjusting for baseline, age, sex
P=0.003 Silence vs. Bowl

PANAS Positive

Table 2, using general linear model for positive PANAS scores and Figure 4 below indicate both groups falling significantly with no difference between baseline and final positive PANAS pre and post in bowl (34.0 to 30.5) versus silence (34.0 to 31.2) groups.

Table 2.

Descriptive Statistics for the Positive PANAS Intervention

Pre/Post	Intervention	Mean	Std. Deviation	N
pospanaspre	a	34.03	7.13	51
	b	34.02	7.76	51
	Total	34.02	7.41	102
pospanaspost	a	31.17	8.84	51
	b	30.49	10.20	51
	Total	30.83	9.51	102

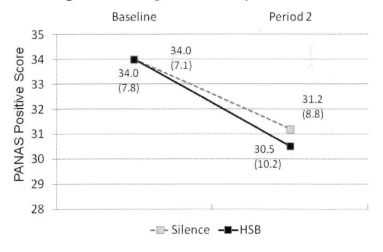

Figure 4: Change in PANAS positive scores

Mean (SD)

PANAS NEGATIVE

Table 3, using general linear model for negative PANAS scores and Figure 5 below indicate both groups falling significantly with greater decrease in bowl group. Although there was no statistically significant difference between the baseline and final negative PANAS pre and negative PANAS post in bowl (13.8 to 10.8) versus silence groups (12.7 to 10.4), the bowl group had a greater decrease in negative scores.

Table 3.

Descriptive Statistics for the Negative PANAS Intervention

Pre/Post	Intervention	Mean	Std. Deviation	N
negpanaspre	a	12.69	3.58	51
	b	13.88	4.99	51
	Total	13.28	4.36	102
negpanaspost	a	10.39	1.15	51
	b	10.78	1.85	51
	Total	10.59	1.54	102

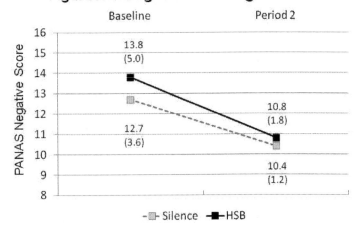

Figure 5: Change in PANAS negative scores

Mean (SD)

Hypertensives

Table 4 illustrates blood pressure values for hypertensives and normotensives on bowl versus silence days.

Table 4.

Blood Pressure Values for Hypertensives and Normotensives

Time Period	Intervention	SBP (mm Hg)		DBP (mm Hg)		HR (per min)	
		NT	HT	NT	HT	NT	HT
Baseline	HBS	124.0	149.1	77.3	87.3	74.5	75.8
		(9.8)	(17.9)	(8.2)	(12.5)	(12.2)	(10.5)
	Silence	120.8	149.7	79.9	89.2	74.1	70.8
		(8.7)	(17.6)	(10.5)	(9.3)	(11.4)	(9.1)
First	HBS	115.5	137.6	75.6	83.4	71.2	71.8
Measurement		(7.7)	(17.0)	(8.9)	(10.3)	(11.7)	(8.5)
	Silence	116.7	140.3	77.3	86.0	69.5	69.5
		(10.8)	(17.9)	(10.1)	(10.0)	(9.8)	(8.4)
Second	HBS	113.8	136.1	76.3	83.8	68.0	69.8
Measurement		(10.2)	(17.8)	(8.9)	(9.6)	(9.5)	(9.1)
	Silence	118.5	140.5	79.7	88.7	70.1	68.6
		(11.5)	(17.2)	(9.2)	(13.0)	(9.8)	(7.5)

Note. Values are mean (SD); NT = normotensive (n = 31); HT = hypertensive (n = 20); SBP = systolic blood pressure; DBP = diastolic blood pressure; HR = heart rate

Systolic BP Comparison of the Hypertensives on Bowl Versus Silence Days

Individuals were defined as hypertensive if systolic BP was greater than 140 mm Hg at the baseline measurement on either session day. Across both interventions, hypertensive individuals (n = 20) had significant changes from baseline in systolic BP when compared to normotensives (n = 31) at both the first measurement (hypertensives: -10.5; normotensives: -6.4 mm Hg; p = 0.012) and second measurement (hypertensives: -11.1;

normotensives: -6.3 mm Hg; $p = 0.017$). There was no significant interaction between hypertensive status and response to the specific interventions. Figures 6 and 7 illustrate systolic BP, in the hypertensives and normotensives in silence (a) and bowl (b) groups. They had the same response between the 2 interventions.

Systolic blood pressure of hypertensives- H (top line)- Hypertensives N=Normal (bottom line).

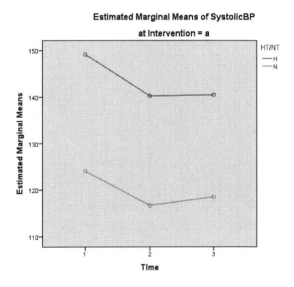

Figure 6. Systolic BP of Hypertensives versus Normotensives with Silence

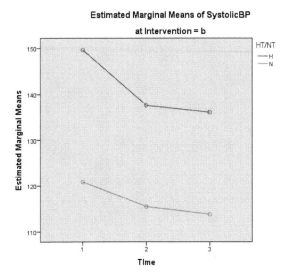

Figure 7. Systolic BP of Hypertensives
vs. Normotensives with Bowl

Diastolic BP Comparison of the Hypertensives on Bowl Versus Silence

Diastolic blood pressure was not significantly different between the groups ($p = .48$) as illustrated by graphs 5 and 6 for silence, versus bowl group. Figures 8 and 9 illustrate diastolic in the hypertensives and normotensives in silence (a) and bowl (b) groups.

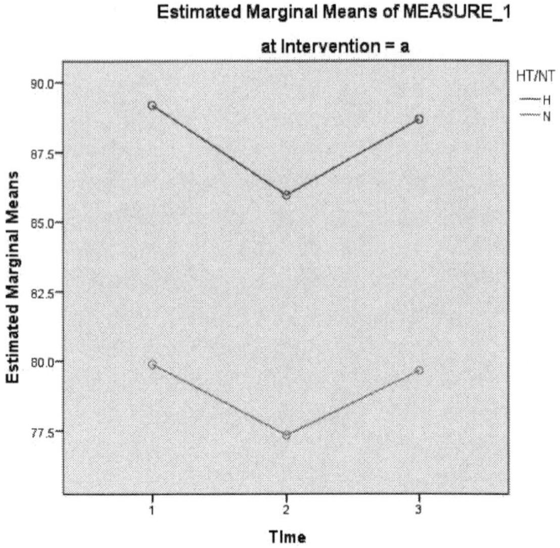

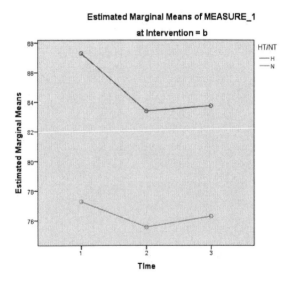

Figure 8. Diastolic BP of Hypertensives
vs. Normotensives with Silence

Figure 9. Diastolic BP of Hypertensives
vs. Normotensives with Bowl

Heart Rate Comparison of the Hypertensives on Bowl Versus Silence Days

Figures 10 and 11 illustrate there was a trend toward a significant difference in response to the two interventions with hypertensives having a greater response ($p = .058$) for heart rate on bowl day versus non bowl day. The hypertensives and normotensives are compared with silence (a) and bowl (b) groups. Figures 10 and 11 illustrate heart rate in the hypertensives and normotensives in silence (a) and bowl (b) groups. In figure 10-H (bottom line)- Hypertensive N=Normal (top line). In figure 11-H (top line)-Hypertensive-N=Normal (bottom line).

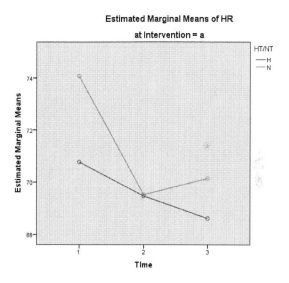

Figure 10. Heart Rate of Hypertensives vs. Normotensives with Silence

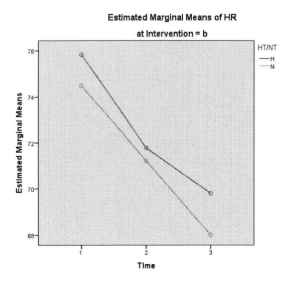

Figure 11. Heart Rate of Hypertensives
vs. Normotensives with Bowl

Participant Responses

Fifty of the fifty-one participants reported feeling more relaxed at the end of both sessions, which included twenty minutes of directed relaxation as a constant. One participant reported feeling the same at the end of both sessions. Forty-eight of fifty-one preferred the bowl session, three preferred silence session.

The following comments describe the stated experiences from participants after data collection on the final session regarding experiences with bowl session unless otherwise specified:

Soothing bowl sound: Three reported the bowl was more soothing than silence.

Bowl & relaxation: Thirty-three reported obtaining deeper, more relaxed state with the bowl.

Sleep states: Although no participants reported falling asleep during the silence session, three *did* fall asleep during the directed relaxation segment of the silence session. During the bowl exposure, one participant reported feeling sleepy, and eight fell asleep as evidenced by snoring and/or presence of rapid eye movement along with reports of dreams. One of the eight that fell asleep did so within the first two minutes of bowl exposure.

Involuntary body movements: When one participant fell asleep during bowl exposure, his right index finger moved involuntarily. Another participant noted her arms were frozen *in a good way.*

Church Associations: Four participants had a positive association with church, while sensing God being present. One used self-guided imagery to walk through the woods and into a chapel where she felt very peaceful and relaxed.

Spiritual: One participant reported traveling *outside his body to another place,* describing it as his deepest, spiritual experience to date, during the bowl session.

Chakras: One participant reported accomplishing important energy work in her crown chakra, while a second described a tingling sensation in her crown chakra. A third described seeing the associated crown chakra colors of purple and blue.

Changes in affect/mind states facilitating relaxation: The researcher made the decision to alternate bowl strike to bowl rub with both running out to silence based on review of literature regarding dynamics of bowl playing (Inacio, 2004; Nur, 2011). Most participants responded favorably to this method ($n = 49$) with two stating the strike segments brought them back up out of a deeper state where they felt *called to attention.* The bowl rub was described as stimulating and calming at the same time, soothing, with the fading sound trailing to silence being very relaxing.

Participants noted feeling more peaceful with the HSB, and described feeling the bowl through their entire body while enjoying the continuity of sound. Other comments included: "I felt beautiful, the energy came up through my feet causing deeper meditation, the bowl helped with internal focus on my body, I loved it, if I were lying down, I'd be asleep, I felt calmer, more chilled out, extreme serene, I felt like I was floating, gave me something to tune into and helped me feel more focused, enabled me to concentrate and relax, I could ignore distracting thoughts and be more clear-minded, when it was over, I felt like I was brought to another place and was in a daze in a *good* way, I felt less stressed, and was slower from the inside out, I could feel the vibrations of the bowl inside my body which was more relaxed than my mind."

Associations with musicians: One participant was a drummer who attained a deeper relaxed state by tuning into the rhythm of the bowl, another, a pianist related to the bowl harmony.

Imagery: Twelve participants reported attaining a deeper meditation state offering imaginary trips from European mountaintops to Paris, including vivid sensations – "the wind was blowing through my hair, and I wanted to live in that peaceful state." Other images during bowl play included seeing clouds, feeling the bowl reverberate *like the ocean*, traveling to the ocean where it is peaceful, and one participant experienced the outside office traffic turning into ocean waves crashing on the beach matching the rhythm of the bowl vibration.

Hypertensives: Three out of five participants were on antihypertensive medication and had a diastolic blood pressure of 90 mm Hg at the end of the second session. These participants were promptly referred to their primary care physician for follow-up evaluation along with nine others who were not diagnosed previously but were hypertensive at completion of session two.

Chapter 4 Summary

In conclusion, results indicated there is a positive relationship between exposure to Himalayan singing bowl HSB and physiological and relaxation responses when used prior to directed relaxation session. The physiological differences were captured using ANOVA and ANCOVA, revealing changes in systolic blood pressure and heart rate, both significantly different with HSB intervention in comparison to silence intervention. Furthermore, there was a significant time x intervention interaction ($p = 0.044$ and $p = 0.003$, respectively). The change in diastolic blood pressure was greater in the HSB group with a non-significant trend ($p = 0.073$). An additional finding included participants who presented with hypertension. When measuring the delta diastolic blood pressure, the hypertensives had the same response between the two interventions. When comparing the hypertensives to normotensives, they had a statistically significant difference in their response (hypertensives + n (.01) no interaction between hypertensives and intervention).

The subjective relaxation experience was captured using the self-administered PANAS scale. General linear model revealed positive PANAS scores falling significantly in both bowl and silence groups with no difference between the baseline and final positive PANAS pre and positive PANAS post in bowl (34.02 to 30.49) versus silence (34.04 to 31.17) groups. Negative PANAS scores fell significantly in both groups with greater decreases in the bowl group. Although there was no statistically significant difference between the baseline and final negative PANAS pre and negative PANAS post in bowl (13.88 to 10.78) versus silence groups (12.69 to 10.39), the bowl group had a greater decrease in negative scores (25% drop in scores from 13 to 10). The clinical implications for the study results will be discussed in greater detail in the final chapter of the dissertation.

CHAPTER 5

CONCLUSIONS AND DISCUSSION

Introduction

The purpose of Chapter Four, was to present study results and a thorough analysis of related data. This chapter will offer an evaluation of the researcher's work while providing personal insight and interpretation. Detailed descriptions include the value of study results for this practitioner, and more broadly, application in the field of psychology and complementary and alternative medicine CAM.

Components include whether the dissertation addressed the need, originally motivating the researcher to create the study. Results will be interpreted in light of previous research findings in the field of relaxation and CAM. Recommendations for future studies will be discussed. Chapter Five outline includes a summary and discussion of results with conclusions in relationship to field literature, limitations, and recommendations for future studies and implications.

Summary of the Results

As explained in Chapter Two, this study was designed to determine the physiological and psychological effects of adding Himalayan singing bowl HSB exposure prior to a meditation practice. The directional hypothesis implied a positive relationship between the use of HSB exposure and enhanced relaxation and positive physiological effects when used prior to directed relaxation DR. This hypothesis guided the study along with the research questions: (1) what are the physiological and relaxation effects when integrating HSB exposure prior to directed relaxation DR session, (2) will the HSB produce an enhanced effect on blood pressure and pulse rate when added prior to DR session versus no HSB exposure prior to meditation session, and (3) will there be an enhanced relaxation experience measuring positive and negative affect (PANAS) with HSB exposure prior to DR session opposed to no HSB exposure prior to DR session.

Literature Review

Literature review included a comprehensive search and study of sound and meditation as it affects physiology. The review started with Pythagoras' early work (c.570-c.495 BC) regarding music theory and its impact on the brain and body through induction of altered mind/body states. Benson's initial (1975) research of the relaxation response was explained and was followed by his later collaborative work with Rossi (2008) in the area of gene expression changes (Dusek et al., 2008). The effects of transcendental meditation TM was explored to determine effects in oxygen, heart rate and theta brain wave changes (Berklie et al., 2003), anxiety and addiction trait reduction (Orme-Johnson & Walton, 1998), cerebral blood flow (Newburg et al., 2003), blood pressure (Anderson et al., 2007; Paul- Labrador et al., 2006; Schneider et al., 2005) and EEG mapping (Gregg et al., 1996).

Additional areas of review included the effects of mindfulness meditation as it relates to positive brain immune function (Davidson et al., 2003), along with tai chi effects on blood pressure (Thomas et al., 2005). Sound therapy was explored offering the effects of chanting (Vilayat, 1982), vibrations (Emoto, 2004), singing (Adero, 2001; Gass & Brehony, 1999), and music on mood, brainwave patterns (Halpern, 1977) and anxiety states (Smith, 2008).

This researcher took the combination of sound and vibration to another level by exploring the possible physiological effects of Himalayan singing bowls. The design and composition (Gaynor, 1995, 2002; Inacio, 2004; Jansen, 1993) along with utilization for relaxed state attainment (Chopra, 1990; Goldman, 2008; Nur, 2011; Seashore, 1937) were considered. Hindu, Sufi and other Eastern philosophies which incorporate the seven major energy centers (chakras) influencing whole body health (Shapiro, 2006) with corresponding musical note scale (Kelly, 2003) were also explained.

Updated Literature Review

A current literature review was completed to determine the presence of new published findings pertinent to this paper, in the areas of altered physiology effects (blood pressure, pulse, heart rate) from relaxation response, TM, CAM, sound and vibration. Search options included full text, peer reviewed and scholarly articles within the past twelve months of study initiation. Stetz et al. (2011) published research including data obtained from three Forward Surgical Teams ($N = 60$) in the military. Three seven-minute video clips of a virtual relaxation (VR) tool (including an embedded guided narrative with imagery), was offered to half the subject group. Results using The State-Trait Anxiety Inventory indicated the VR tool was successful in reducing overall anxiety levels. Physiological measurements were not assessed. Rosenthal, Grosswald, Ross, and Rosenthal (2011) published research along a similar line, using transcendental meditation TM taught to veterans of Operation Enduring Freedom (OEF) and Operation Iraqi Freedom (OIF), from eighteen to sixty-five years of age with a history of moderately severe combat-related PTSD. Subjects agreed to practice the TM technique for twenty minutes twice a day for three months. Efficacy of treatment was assessed using the Clinician Administered PTSD Scale (CAPS). Secondary outcome measures included the PTSD Checklist-Military Version (PCL-M), the Quality of Life Enjoyment and Satisfaction Questionnaire (Q-LES-Q), Clinical Global Impression-Improvement (CGI-I) scales, the Clinical Global Impression-Severity (CGI-S) and the Beck Depression Inventory (BDI). Although the pilot study had a small ($n = 5$), sample size and was uncontrolled, TM may have helped alleviate symptoms of PTSD and improve quality of life in the veterans who had combat-related PTSD.

Wright, Gregorski, Tinge, and Trieber (2011) examined the impact of breathing awareness meditation (BAM), life skills (LS) training, and health education (HE) interventions on self-reported hostility and 24-hour ambulatory blood pressure (ABP) in 121 African Americans (AA). Their sample included ninth graders who demonstrated an increased risk for essential hypertension development. Participants were randomly assigned to BAM, LS, or HE and participated in these intervention sessions during health class for three months. After the intervention ended, self-reported hostility and ABP were measured before, after, and three months following. Results indicated between pre and post intervention, BAM participants had significant decreases in self-reported hostility along with 24-hour systolic ABP.

Gregorski, Barnes, Tingen, Harshfield, and Treiber (2011) evaluated the effects of a breathing awareness meditation (BAM), Botvin Life Skills Training (LST), and health education control (HEC) on ambulatory blood pressure (ABP) and sodium excretion in African American adolescents (N=166). After three days of systolic blood pressure (SBP) measurements, the participants were randomly assigned to BAM (n=53), LST (n=69), or HEC (n=44). The intervention sessions were held at school and offered for three months by health education teachers. Overnight urine samples and 24-hour ambulatory SBP, diastolic blood pressure, and heart rate were obtained pre and post interventions. Results indicated significant group differences in overnight SBP, diastolic blood pressure, and heart rate over the 24-hour period and during school hours with BAM group exhibiting the greatest decreases. There was a non-significant trend for overnight urinary sodium excretion (p= .07), with BAM group displaying a reduction of -.92 ± 1.1 mEq/hr compared with increases of .89 ± 1.2 mEq/hr for LST and .58 ± .9 mEq/hr for HEC group. Thus BAM improved hemodynamic function by affecting sodium handling among African American adolescents at risk for development of cardiovascular disease.

Akiyama and Sutoo (2011) explored the effects of music frequency on brain function. Using spontaneously hypertensive laboratory rats (SHR), different frequencies of music on brain function were investigated by measuring blood pressure.

Using Mozart's music (K.205) the study demonstrated blood pressure reducing response was dependent on the frequency, and was markedly greater at 4k-16k Hz compared with lower frequencies. The findings suggest that music containing high frequency sounds stimulate dopamine synthesis, which may affect various brain functions.

In the area of mindfulness based stress reduction (MBSR), Matchim, Armer, and Stewart (2011) reported a statistically significant improvement in physiological and psychological outcomes including reduced blood pressure, heart rate, and respiratory rate along with increased mindfulness state at the level of $p = 0.05$ to $p = 0.001$. Subjects included early stage breast cancer survivors and consisted of a quasi-experimental, pre and post test control group design. The intervention group received the MBSR and the control group did not receive MBSR. The effect was not sustained at a one-month follow up. In a different study conducted by Campbell, Labelle and Bacon (2011), female post cancer treatment patients were recruited from MBSR program. Participants completed self-report measures on mindfulness and rumination, and measured blood pressure at home before and after their eight-week MBSR program. This group was compared to those in a waiting period. Results indicated the MBSR group demonstrated higher levels of mindful-attentiveness, lower rumination, and decreases in systolic blood pressure ($n = 19$) compared to control group ($n = 16$) by the end of the eighth week.

Methodology

In this study, the quantitative research method was used to measure physiological effects (systolic/diastolic blood pressures and heart rate) as well as psychological effects (self-administered

PANAS) comparing HSB exposure to silence prior to a twenty-minute directed relaxation session. Results of the correlational design were obtained by statistical analysis using IBM-SPSS version 20 and Sigmastat by Jandel Corporation (1994). ANOVA Two Way, measures analysis of variance on two factors using a balanced design. This general linear model analysis for repeated measures allows the same person to serve as their own control. ANCOVA was implemented to adjust for the introduction of parameters such as baseline readings, age and sex and their effect on physiology over time.

Findings

Fifty-six adult participants ranging in age from twenty-six to sixty-nine, responded to the study, with a total of fifty-one (sixteen male and thirty-five female) completing both sessions within a few weeks period of time ($N = 102$ sessions). Data from the incomplete sets (five) were not utilized. Findings supported the directional hypothesis: there was a positive relationship between the use of HSB exposure and enhanced relaxation, with positive physiological effects when used prior to directed relaxation DR compared to the same session using silence. There was a statistically significant drop in systolic and diastolic blood pressures over time in both interventions with the bowl group having a sustained fall compared to the silence group. Heart rate fell in a similar pattern to blood pressures. Hypertensive individuals had the same response between the two interventions, but when compared to the normotensives, the hypertensives had a statistically significant difference in their response to the HSB session.

Self-administered PANAS results indicated bowl and silence interventions produced significant decreases in scores, with no statistically significant difference between the two.

The relaxation response from the session resulted in a fall of both positive measures (interested, excited, strong, enthusiastic, proud, alert, inspired, determined, attentive, active), as well as negative measures (distressed, upset, guilty, scared hostile, irritable, ashamed, nervous, jittery, afraid).

Discussion of the Results

The study results supported the original hypothesis and research questions by demonstrating both physiologic and relaxation effects of Himalayan singing bowl HSB exposure. When HSB is added to a meditation session, there is an enhanced physiological effect resulting in a deeper relaxation response. Fifty out of fifty-one participants reported feeling more relaxed at the end of both sessions, which included the twenty-minutes of directed relaxation as a constant.

Results suggest that HSB exposure has the potential to create a deeper meditative experience and decrease negative affect states. This positive relationship between Himalayan singing bowl HSB exposure and physiological and relaxation responses was evident in statistically significant differences in systolic blood pressure ($p = 0.044$) and heart rate ($p = 0.003$) change with the HSB session over silence session. Changes in diastolic blood pressure were also greater in the HSB group with a non-significant trend ($p = 0.073$). There was also an enhanced response to the HSB by participants who presented with hypertension. When this group was compared to normotensives, there was a statistically significant difference in their response. Thus, HSB exposure could be used as an adjunct to other complementary and alternative medicine techniques to acutely lower blood pressure, particularly in hypertensive individuals. What is not known from the present study is the duration of the effect.

When looking at the subjective relaxation experience, captured by the self-administered PANAS scale, participants had a significant drop in both positive and negative affect states. Based on prior studies in the area of relaxation response, it is plausible that negative states (distressed, upset, guilty, scared, hostile, irritable, ashamed, nervous, jittery, and afraid) would fall during the relaxation response. This indeed happened and scores fell significantly with both interventions but with greater decrease in the HSB group. But the analyses also showed both positive and negative states falling in parallel. The fact that positive states (interested, excited, strong, enthusiastic, proud, alert, inspired, determined, attentive, and active) fell as well may have been due to enhanced relaxation achieved during the interventions. This likely resulted from the participant being in a very relaxed meditative or sleep state, by the session's end. The study demonstrated when an individual relaxes with HSB it results in a fall of positive and negative affect measures. Therefore, the PANAS may not have been the ideal instrument to capture enhanced positive changes in the subjective experience during this experiment.

In light of the intense and varied participant responses, it would be interesting to design and implement a qualitative study to explore personal experiences with HSB exposure in greater detail. Nearly all the participants preferred the HSB session to the silence session. This may be relevant to its utility as a treatment tool with certain clients.

Two participants experienced involuntary movements: one moved her right index finger, and another, described her arms felt *frozen in a good way*. Ogden (2000) has identified the presence of involuntary micro movements and gestures consistent with sensorimotor processing which can occur spontaneously during the body's processing of prior trauma experiences. In the absence of cognitive processing, this interactive regulation can have a positive effect on emotions. Van der Kolk (1996) describes the origin of these unresolved sensorimotor reactions as part of the conditional emotional and cognitive processing system, which if unresolved, can lead to a disruption in the traumatized person's ability to think clearly or to glean accurate information from emotional states. Levine (2000) offers another way to understand involuntary movements as *organic discharge*, for explicit memory is accessed primarily through implicit memory, which is reached through the body. This *felt* sense, enables non-conscious intentional movement to facilitate the release of bound energy leading to renegotiation and healing of trauma. It is possible HSB exposure has implications for somatic experiencing in this body-oriented psychotherapy approach.

It is helpful to consider the HSB as an inverted bell without a striker. When struck with the puja, it offers a superior bell resonance. Some participants identified the bell sound of HSB with positive church and chapel associations. That included feeling God's presence in the bowl session, contributing to a very peaceful and more relaxed feeling state. Two musicians noted a deeper relaxed state by tuning into the rhythm of the bowl, and relating to bowl harmony.

Other spiritual experiences noted by participants included specific references to the crown chakra. This latter observation was interesting since the Bb bowl tone designation of the HSB used for the study was not discussed with any participant. The tone is associated with the crown chakra on the musical note scale (Kelly, 2003). Study participants did not mention any of the other six chakras.

Discussion of Conclusions

This research project studied CAM technique using a purely Western approach. Results determined that introducing HSB prior to a meditation session did indeed promote an enhanced relaxation response as evidenced by statistically significant decreases in systolic/diastolic blood pressures, heart rate, and negative affect scores. The study builds upon prior research in the fields of meditation and music therapy and bridges the gap between the efficacy of sound in the form of HSB and its physiologic and enhanced relaxation effects. Results presented support and confirm the positive physiological and relaxation effects when incorporating HSB into a meditation session. These results have broad implications in the wider field of psychology and mental health for both the traditional Western medical community and the Eastern complementary and alternative medicine community CAM.

Experts estimate that up to seventy-five percent of fatigue and medical disorders are directly attributable to stress (Hughes et al., 1984; Kaptein et al., 1990). Medical problems develop when one lives in chronic stress states, potentially related to cortisol and adrenaline stress hormone release. These psychosocial stressors and stress hormones can lead to hypertension (Weiner, 1977) cardiac disease (Hanser, 1985), gastrointestinal problems (Khorana, 1983), and migraines (Steven & Shanahan, 2002). The present study builds upon the initial work of Benson's (1975) *relaxation response*. A number of studies thirty years hence have demonstrated the physical and mental health benefits of deeper relaxation, meditation, mindfulness, and music therapy. Having this knowledge offers clinicians another tool to help minimize the impact of stressors on illness and disease causation.

Limitations

Several limitations may have affected both the results of the study and its generalizability. The rationale for using the PANAS was to determine the subjective relaxation states comparing HSB to silence sessions. The use of PANAS for relaxation assessment could be viewed as a limitation of the study, as the participants reported some opposites of positive (i.e. interested, inspired, strong, alert), when being aroused from such a deeply relaxed state. The goal was to measure an increased feeling of relaxation and this tool was not designed entirely for that purpose. In future studies, I would recommend a tool designed specifically for capturing relaxation levels.

The sample size along with a lack of cultural variety in participants may also be a limitation. It is uncertain whether a study repeated with a larger sample would yield similar results. Observations that hypertensives had a greater response to HSB, although intriguing and noteworthy, were drawn from a subset of the participants and were not a pre-specified analysis. Similar studies with a larger sample of hypertensive individuals would add to the body of literature regarding their response to HSB exposure.

Age and cultural backgrounds of participants may be limitations to the study. The majority of the population ranged in age from twenty-six to sixty-nine. The mean age of participants was 50.5. Based on the mean age of the sample, conclusions may not represent how a younger or older participant would respond to a similar study.

The relatively homogeneous race and ethnicity of study population is reflective of 96.1% white, native-born occupants in the municipality the study was conducted. Even though the researcher exercised great care to observe and document with objectivity, results may be influenced by the researcher's similar cultural background to most participants.

According to Kirmayer (2001), the clinician can see the client through his or her own lens which may include training, cultural experiences and current setting, thus creating an intracultural therapeutic exchange. Social and cultural contexts must be considered before one could make associations about how other cultures would respond to the same study.

Another limitation could be the use of this particular B^b metal HSB. Since the bowl is handmade from the Nepal region, it might be considered a challenge to replicate the study without the exact bowl. It would be very interesting to do a similar study with other handmade bowls of differing sizes and tones. Another idea would be to replicate this study using a crystal bowl of the same B^b tone to determine similarities or differences in results. Since the two bowls are made of different compositions, it would not be appropriate to make the same assumptions about the results of this study regarding the efficacy of crystal singing bowls.

It is also very possible that study results were affected by either the Hawthorne effect or regression to the mean. The idea that human self-awareness may influence clinical investigation results is well established. In considering the Hawthorne effect, when human subjects know they are being studied, that knowledge may in fact influence their behavior. As such, participants may try to respond as they think the researcher expects them to (Comer, 2007). It's also possible that the attention the participant received during the twelve-minute bowl session versus being left alone in the room during the silence session may have increased optimism, improved mood and affected responses.

Recommendations for Further Research or Intervention

While a single quantitative study cannot provide a sound basis for changes in the practice of relaxation response, this study suggests that adding HSB has a positive effect on physiology and relaxation. It is hoped results will spur further research on the impact of sound and vibration with HSB and stress management. In addition, creating or finding a tool to assess affective functioning with construct validity and reliability specifically assessing positive relaxation states would be helpful.

Future studies could be conducted using patients with hypertension. The relaxation approach implemented in this study could have positive ramifications for the hypertensive population. The technique of playing the bowl is simple and this form of therapy is inexpensive, portable and carries no foreseeable risks.

Further studies using HSB could advance the psychotherapeutic area of somatic experiencing and sensorimotor processing. Somatic experiencing encompasses education and body-oriented psychotherapy including the interconnection between body, brain and mind. Traumatized individuals learn to restore homeostasis after being aroused by a threat. Once implicit traumatic memory is accessed in a resourced way (through felt sense such as involuntary movements), it is transformed and changes. This change leads to healing. Involuntary movements by participants were noted during the study and may have been indicative of traumatic healing through sensorimotor reprocessing.

Practitioners might consider incorporating a B[b] HSB in their practice to enhance deeper relaxation and meditative states. Knowledge gained from future studies combining

Eastern and Western approaches would advance best practices in the field of meditation and relaxation and improve mental and physical well-being in the clients served.

Conclusion

Study results indicated a positive relationship between the use of HSB exposure and enhanced relaxation. In addition, positive physiological effects occurred when HSB was used prior to directed relaxation DR. Conclusions drawn from data analysis contribute to the body of knowledge in the area of relaxation response and music therapy. The bowl is easy to play, carries low risk, is inexpensive, portable and can be taught to clients as a technique aiding in self-care. These findings have a significant impact on and can change practices for clinicians assisting clients with various relaxation needs. Incorporating this tool prior to a meditation session enhances the relaxation response, an essential component of stress management. This leads to an improvement in physical and mental well-being offering a deeper quality of life.

DISSERTATION REFERENCES

Abbott, A. (2008). The Brains of the Family. *Nature, 454,* 154-157.

Adero, M. (2001). Mindbodysoul. *Essence, 32*(1), 90.

Akiyama, K., & Sutoo, D. (2011). Effect of Different Frequencies of Music on Blood Pressure Regulation in Spontaneously Hypertensive Rats. *Neuroscience Letters, 487*(1), 58-60.

Anderson, J., Liu, C., & Kryscio, R. (2008). Blood Pressure Response to Transcendental Meditation: A Meta-Analysis. *American Journal of Hypertension, 21,* 310-316.

Andover demographics. (n.d.). Retrieved from http://www. zillow.com/local-info/MA-Andover- people/r_43900.

Benson, H. (1975). *The Relaxation Response.* New York, NY: HarperCollins.

Bjerklie, D., Park, A., Van Biema, D., Cullotta, K., McDowell, J., & Stein, J. (2003). Just Say Om. *Time International (Canada Edition), 162*(5), 38-46.

Campbell, T. S., Labelle, L. E., & Bacon, S. L., Faris, P., & Carlson, L. E. (2011). Impact of Mindfulness-Based Stress Reduction (MBSR) on Attention, Rumination and Resting Blood Pressure in Woman with Cancer: A Waitlist-Controlled Study. *Journal of Behavioral Medicine.* doi:10.1007/510865-001-9357-1.

Chopra, D. (1990). *Quantum Healing.* New York, NY: Bantam Books.

Comer, R. J. (2007). *Abnormal Psychology* (6th ed.). New York, NY: Worth.

Conlin, P. (2008). Nonpharmacologic treatment. In C. Wilcox C (ed.), *Therapy of Nephrology and Hypertension: A Companion to Brenner and Rector's the Kidney* (3rd ed.) (pp. 75- 150). Philadelphia, PA: Harcourt Health Sciences.

Crawford, J., & Henry, J. (2004). The Positive and Negative Affect Schedule (PANAS): Construct Validity, Measurement Properties and Normative Data in a Large Non-Clinical Sample. *British Journal of Psychological Society, 43*, 245-265.

Davidson, R., Kabat-Zinn, J., Schumacher, J., Rosenkranz, M., Muller, D., Santorelli, F., Urbanowski, F., Harrington, A., Bonus, K., & Sheridan, J. (2003). Alterations in Brain and Immune Function Produced by Mindfulness Meditation. *Psychosomatic Medicine, 65*, 564-570.

Dusek, J., Hasan, H., Wohlhueter, A., Bhasin, M., Zerbini, L., Joseph, M., Benson, H., & Libermann, T. (2008). Genomic Counter-Stress Changes Induced by the Relaxation Response. *Plos One, 3*(7): e2576. doi:10.1371/journal.pone.0002576.

Eisen, M., Spellman, P., Brown, P., & Botstein, D. (1998). Cluster Analysis and Display of Genome-Wide Expression Patterns. *Proceedings of the National Academy of Sciences, 95*, 14863-14868.

Emoto, M. (2004). *The Hidden Messages in Water.* Hillsboro, OR: Beyond Words.

Gall, M. D., Borg, W. R., & Gall, J. P. (2003). *Educational Research: Introduction* (7th ed.).New York, NY: Longman.

Gardner, K. (1990). *Sounding the Inner Landscape: Music as Medicine.* Rockport, MA: Element.

Gass, R., & Brehony, K. (1999). *Chanting: Discovering Spirit in Sound.* New York, NY: Broadway Books.

Gaynor, M. L. (1999). *Sounds of Healing: A Physician Reveals the Therapeutic Power of Sound, Voice, and Music.* New York, NY: Bantam Dell Group.

Gaynor, M. L. (2002). *The Healing Power of Sound: Recovery from Life-Threatening Illness using Sound, Voice and Music.* Boston, MA: Shambhala Publications.

Glatthorn, A., & Joyner, R. (2005). *Writing the Winning Dissertation: A Step-by-Step Guide* (2nd ed.). Thousand Oaks, CA: Corwin.

Goldman, J. (2008). *The Seven Secrets of Sound Healing.* New York, NY: Hay House, Inc.

Gregg, D., Jacobs, G., & Benson, H. (1996). Topographic EEG Mapping of the Relaxation Response. *Biofeedback and Self-Regulation, 21*(2), 125-132.

Gregoski, B., Barnes, V., Tingen, M., Harshfield, G., & Treiber, F. (2011). Breathing Awareness Meditation and Life Skills Training Programs Influence upon Ambulatory Blood Pressure and Sodium Excretion Among African American Adolescents. *Journal of Adolescent Health, 48*(1), 59-64.

Halpern, S. (1977). *Tuning the Human Instrument.* New York, NY: Harper & Row.

Hanser, S. B. (1985). Music Therapy and Stress Reduction Research. *Journal of Music Therapy, 22*(4), 193-206.

Heide, F. J., & Borkovec, T. D. (1984). Relaxation-Induced Anxiety: Mechanisms and Theoretical Implications. *Behaviour Research and Therapy, 22*, 1–12.

Hughes, G., Pearson, M., & Reinhart, G. (1984). Stress: Sources, Effects and Management. *Family and Community Health, 7*(1), 47-55.

Huyser, A. (1999). *Singing Bowl Exercises for Personal Harmony.* Havelete, Holland: Binkey Kok Publications.

Inácio, J. (2004). Dynamical Responses of a Large Tibetan Singing Bowl. *Proceedings of the International Symposium on Musical Acoustics, Nara: Japan.*

Kabat-Zinn, J. (1990). *Full Catastrophe Living: Using the Wisdom of your Body and Mind to Face Stress, Pain, and Illness.* New York, NY: Delta.

Kabat-Zinn, J., Massion, A., & Kristeller, J. (1992). Effectiveness of a Meditation-Based Stress Reduction Program in the Treatment of Anxiety Disorders. *American Journal of Psychiatry, 149,* 936–943.

Kabat-Zinn, J. (1994). *Wherever You Go, There You Are: Mindfulness Meditation in Everyday Life.* New York, NY: Hyperion.

Kaptein, A., Van der Ploeg, H. M., Carseen, B., & Beunderman, R. (1990). *Behavioral Medicine: Psychological Treatment of Somatic Disorders.* Chechester, NY: John Wiley & Sons.

Kelly, R. (2003). Sacred Sound Therapy for Healing, Spiritual Growth and Meditation. *Positive Health, 93,* 13-16.

Khorana, S. (1983). A Study of Psychological Factors and Psychotherapy on Ulcerative Colitis. *Indian Journal of Clinical Psychology, 10,* 459-468.

Kirmayer, L. (2001). Cultural Variations in the Clinical Presentation of Depression and Anxiety: Implications for Diagnosis and Treatment. *Journal of Clinical Psychiatry, 62*(13), 22-28.

Kristeller, J., & Hallett, C. (1999). An Exploratory Study of a Meditation Based Intervention for Binge Eating Disorder. *Journal of Health Psychology, 4,* 357–363.

Lazarus, A. A. (1984). The Specificity Factor in Psychotherapy. *Psychotherapy in Private Practice, 2,* 43–48.

Lazarus, A. A., & Mayne, T. J. (1990). Relaxation: Some Limitations, Side Effects, and Proposed Solutions.

Psychotherapy: Theory, Research, Practice, Training, 27(2), 261-266.

Lehrer, P. M., Hochron, S. M., McCann, B., Swartzman, L., & Reba, P. (1986). Relaxation Decreases Large-Airway but not Small-Airway Asthma. *Journal of Psychosomatic Research, 30*, 13–25.

Levine, P. (1997). *Waking the Tiger, Healing Trauma: The Innate Capacity to Transform Overwhelming Experiences.* Berkley, CA: North Atlantic Books.

Linehan M. (1993). *Cognitive-Behavioral Treatment of Borderline Personality Disorder.* New York, NY: Guilford.

Lord, S., & Hylton, M. (2002). Physiologic, Psychologic and Health Predictors of 6-Minute Walk Performance in Older People. *Archives of Physical Medicine and Rehabilitation, 83*, 907- 911.

Martin, W. H. (1924). The Transmission Unit and Telephone Transmission Reference Systems. *Bell System Technical Journal, 43*, 797-801.

Matchim, Y., Armer, J., & Stewart, B. (2011). Effects of Mindfulness Based Stress Reduction (MBSR) on Health Among Breast Cancer Survivors. *Western Journal of Nursing Research, 33*(8), 996-1016.

Mayberg, H., Lozano, A., Voon, V., McNeely, H., Seminowicz, D., Hamani, C. Schwalb, J. M., & Kennedy, S. H. (2005). Deep Brain Simulation for Treatment-Resistant Depression. *Neuron, 45*, 651-660.

Middleton, W., Harris, P., & Surman, M. (1996). Give 'Em Enough Rope: Perception of Health and Safety Risks in Bungee Jumpers. *Journal of Social and Clinical Psychology, 15*(1), 68- 79.

Nestler, E. (2008). A Psychiatrist Talks about Finding Answers That Add Up Across All Levels. *Nature, 451*, 1033.

Newburg, A., Pourdehnad, A., & O'Aquili, E. G. (2003). Cerebral Blood Flow During Meditative Prayer: Preliminary Findings and Methodological Issues. *Perceptual and Motor Skills, 97,* 625-630.

Nur, M. (2006). 2006 classes with Mitch Nur. Retrieved from http://nineways.tripod.com/2005classeswithmitchnur/id11html.

Ogden, P., & Minton, K. (2000). Sensorimotor Psychotherapy: One Method for Processing Traumatic Memory. *Traumatology, 6*(3), 3.

Orme-Johnson, D. W., & Walton, K. (1998). All Approaches to Preventing and Reversing the Effects of Stress are Not the Same. *American Journal of Health Promotion, 12,* 297–299.

Paul-Labrador, M., Polk, D., Dwyer, J., Velasquez, I., Nidich, S., Rainforth, M., Schneider, R., & Merz, M. B. (2006). Effects of a Randomized Controlled Trial of Transcendental Meditation on Components of the Metabolic Syndrome in Subjects with Coronary Artery Disease. *Archives of Internal Medicine, 166,* 1218-1224.

Prochazka, H. (2004). Pythagoras' Music. *Australian Mathematics Teacher, 60*(4), 10.

Roberts, K., Dimsdale, J., East, P., & Friedman, L. (1998). Adolescent Emotional Response to Music and its Relationship to Risk-taking Behaviors. *Journal of Adolescent Health, 23,* 49- 54.

Rosenthal, J., Grosswald, S., Ross, R., & Rosenthal, N. (2011). Effects of Transcendental Meditation in Veterans of Operation Enduring Freedom and Operation Iraqi Freedom with Post Traumatic Stress Disorder: A Pilot Study. *Military Medicine, 176*(6), 626-30.

Rossi, E. R. (1986). *The Psychobiology of Mind-Body Healing: New Concepts of Therapeutic Hypnosis* (2nd ed.), New York, NY: W. W. Norton.

Rossi, E. R., & Rossi, K. L. (1988). *The New Neuroscience of Psychotherapy, Therapeutic Hypnosis & Rehabilitation: A Creative Dialogue with our Genes.* A Free Book retrieved from http://www.ErnestRossi.com.

Rossi, E. R. (2002). *The Psychobiology of Gene Expression: Neuroscience and Neurogenesis in Therapeutic Hypnosis and the Healing Arts.* NewYork, NY: W. W. Norton Professional Books.

Rossi, E. R. (2004). Translator & Editor, Salvador Iannotti. *A Discourse with Our Genes: The Psychosocial and Cultural Genomics of Therapeutic Hypnosis and Psychotherapy.* Benevento, Italy: Editris SAS Press.

Rossi, E. R. (2005). Prospects for Exploring the Molecular-Genomic Foundations of Therapeutic Hypnosis with DNA Microarrays. *American Journal of Clinical Hypnosis, 48,* 165-182.

Rossi, E. R., Rossi, K. L., Yount, G., Cozzolino, M., & Iannotti, S. (2006). The Bioinformatics of Integrative Medical Insights: Proposals for an International Psychosocial and Cultural Bioinformatics Project. *Integrative Medicine Insights, 2,* 1-19.

Rossi, E. R. (2007). *The Breakout Heuristic: The New Neuroscience of Mirror Neurons, Consciousness and Creativity in Human Relationship.* Phoenix, AZ: The Milton H. Erickson Foundation Press.

Rossi, E. R., Iannotti, S., Cozzolino, M., Castiglione, S., Cicatelli, A., & Rossi, K. (2008). A Pilot Study of Positive Expectations and Focused Attention via a New Protocol for Optimizing Therapeutic Hypnosis and Psychotherapy

Assessed with DNA Microarrays: The Creative Psychosocial Genomic Healing Experience. *Sleep and Hypnosis, 10,* 1-9.

Rossi, E. R., & Rossi, K. L. (2008). Open Questions on Mind, Genes, Consciousness, and Behavior: The Circadian and Ultradian Rhythms of Art, Beauty, and Truth in Creativity. In L. Rossi (ed.) *Ultradian Rhythms from Molecule to Mind: A New Vision of Life* (pp. 391-412). New York, NY: Springer.

Salerno, J., Sheppard, W., Castillo-Richmond, A., Barnes, V., & Nidich, S. (2005). A Randomized Controlled Trial of Stress Reduction in African Americans Treated for Hypertension Over One Year. *American Journal of Hypertension, 18,* 88-98.

Schneider, R., Alexander, C., Staggers, F., Rainforth, M., Salerno, J., Hartz, A., Arndt, S., Barnes, V. A., & Nidich, S. I. (2005). Long-Term Effects of Stress Reduction on Mortality in Persons > or = 55 Years of Age with Systemic Hypertension. *American Journal Cardiology, 95*(9), 1060-1064.

Seashore, C. (1937). The Psychology of Music. *Music Educators Journal, 23*(6), 28-29.

Selye, H. (1982). *Handbook of Stress: Theoretical and Clinical Aspects* (2nd ed.). New York, NY:Free Press.

Shapiro, D. (2006). *Your Body Speaks Your Mind.* Boulder, CO: Sounds True, Inc.

Smith, J. C. (2001). *Advances in ABC Relaxation Training: Applications and Inventories.* New York, NY: Springer Publishing Company.

Smith, J. C., & Joyce, C.A. (2004). Mozart Versus New Age Music: Relaxation States, Stress, and ABC Relaxation Theory. *Journal of Music Therapy, 41*(3), 215-24.

Smith, M. (2008). The Effects of a Single Music Relaxation Session on State Anxiety Levels of Adults in a Workplace

Environment. *The Australian Journal of Music Therapy, 19,* 45-66.

Steinberg, R. (2011). *Mindfulness, Psychological Well-Being, and Rock Climbing: An Exploration of Mindfulness in Rock Climbers and the Potential for Psychological Benefit* (Unpublished Doctoral Dissertation). The Wright Institute.

Stetz, M. C., Kaloi-Chen, J. Y., Turner, D. D., Bouchard, S., Riva, G., & Wiederhold, B. K. (2011). The Effectiveness of Technology-Enhanced Relaxation Techniques for Military Medical Warriors. *Military Medicine, 176*(9), 1065-1070.

Steven, I. D., & Shanahan, E. M. (2002). Work-Related Stress: Care and Compensation. *Medical Journal of Australia, 176,* 363-365.

The Transcendental Meditation Program. (n.d.). Retrieved from http://www.tm.org/tuition.

Thomas, G., Hong, A., Tomlinson, B., Lau, E., Lam, C., Sanderson, J., & Woo, J. (2005). Effects of Tai Chi and Resistance Training on Cardiovascular Risk Factors in Elderly Chinese Subjects: A 12-Month Longitudinal, Randomized, Controlled Intervention Study. *Clinical Endocrinology, 63,* 663-669.

Thompson, E. (2007). Development and Validation of an Internationally Reliable Short-Form of the Positive and Negative Affect Schedule (PANAS). *Journal of Cross-Cultural Psychology,* 38(3), 227-242.

Tiller, W. (2005). What the Bleep Do We Know!?: A Personal Narrative. *Vision in Action (VIA), 2*(3-4), 16-20.

Van der Kolk, B. A. (1996*). The Body Keeps the Score; Approaches to the Psychobiology of Post Traumatic Stress Disorder.* New York, NY: Guilford.

Vilayat, P. (1982). *Introducing Spirituality into Counseling and Therapy.* Santa Fe, NM: Omega Press.

Vollmer, W. M., Appel, L., Svetkey, L., Moore, T., Vogt, T. M., Conlin, P. R., Proschan, M. & Harsha, D. (2005) Comparing Office-Based and Ambulatory Blood Pressure Monitoring in Clinical Trials. *Journal Human Hypertension,* 19, 77-82.

Wang, C., Collet, J., & Lau, J. (2004). The Effects of Tai Chi on Health Outcomes in Patient with Chronic conditions: A Systematic Review. *Archives of Internal Medicine, 164,* 493-501.

Watson, D., Clark, L. A., & Tellegen, A. (1988). Development and Validation of Brief Measures of Positive and Negative Affect: The PANAS Scales. *Journal of Personality and Social Psychology, 54*(6), 1063-1070.

Watson, D., & Walker, L. (1996). The Long-Term Stability and Predictive Validity of Trait Measures of Affect. *Journal of Personality and Social Psychology, 70*(3), 567-577.

Weiner, H. (1977). *Psychobiology and Human Disease.* New York, NY: Elsevier.

Wright, L. Gregoski, M., Tingen, M., Barnes, V., & Treiber, F. (2011). Impact of Stress Reduction Interventions on Hostility and Ambulatory Systolic Blood Pressure in African American adolescents. *The Journal of Black Psychology, 37*(2), 210-233.

Zevon, M. A., & Tellegen, A. (1982). The Structure of Mood Change: An Idiographic/Nomotheticanalysis. *Journal of Personality and Social Psychology, 43,* 111–122.

APPENDIX A.
DIRECTED RELAXATION SCRIPT

Partial Twenty-Minute Directed Relaxation DR Script©
For Doctoral Dissertation
Author: Jayan Landry MS, APRN-BC
(Script will be recorded in advance and
played for study participants).

Get comfortable in your seated position moving your body and using the cushions to provide maximum support.

Know that when you take this time over the next twenty minutes to clear your mind, you will be helping your body and mind become more relaxed.

Being in this relaxed state is good for your mind and body.

Now if you are comfortable, close your eyes to minimize distractions and place your hands on your lower belly.

Picture breathing into your front and back lungs as you inhale through your nose. As you inhale, puff out your lower abdomen like a balloon, feeling your hands rise over your lower belly.

Inhale through your nose, puffing out your belly, exhale with your lips slightly open. Push the air through the back of your throat making the sound "her," drawing out the *e*.

Inhale through your nose, puffing out your belly, exhale through the back of your throat.

"HER"

Inhale through your nose, puffing out your belly, exhale through the back of your throat.

"HER"

Inhale through your nose, puffing out your belly, exhale through the back of your throat.

"HER"

When you exhale, make the sound "her" with the back of your throat. The motion is similar to *fogging up* a mirror held close to your lips. This is called ujjayi breathing or *ocean sounding breath*. Think of the *Darth Vader* sound when you exhale.

Inhale through your nose, puffing out your belly, exhale through the back of your throat.

"HER"

Inhale through your nose, puffing out your belly, exhale through the back of your throat.

"HER"

Inhale through your nose, puffing out your belly, exhale through the back of your throat.

"HER"

Inhale through your nose, puffing out your belly, exhale through the back of your throat.

"HER"

Inhale through your nose, puffing out your belly, exhale through the back of your throat.

"HER"

When you breathe in this way, the "her" stimulates the top of the 10th cranial nerve which innervates the parasympathetic nervous system running straight from the throat through the center of your chest reducing your heart and respiratory rate. In addition, stomach nerves are soothed. The opposite happens when we are stressed. Breathing in this way helps relax our central nervous system eliciting the parasympathetic (calm you down) branch. This is very helpful to our body and allows us to think more clearly.

Inhale through your nose, puffing out your belly, exhale through the back of your throat.

"HER"

Inhale through your nose, puffing out your belly, exhale through the back of your throat.

"HER"

Inhale through your nose, puffing out your belly, exhale through the back of your throat.

"HER"

Inhale through your nose, puffing out your belly, exhale through the back of your throat.

"HER"

And as you breathe in, picture a clear blue sky.

Inhale through your nose, puffing out your belly, exhale through the back of your throat.

"HER"

Inhale through your nose, puffing out your belly, exhale through the back of your throat.

"HER"

If a thought enters your mind, think of the thought as a cloud. Just be an observer of the cloud, and allow the wind to blow the cloud across your clear blue sky and out of view.

Return to thinking about your clear blue sky.

Inhale through your nose, puffing out your belly, exhale through the back of your throat.

"HER"

Inhale through your nose, puffing out your belly, exhale through the back of your throat.

"HER"

Inhale through your nose, puffing out your belly, exhale through the back of your throat.

"HER"

Inhale through your nose, puffing out your belly, exhale through the back of your throat.

"HER"

As these distracting thoughts enter your mind, do not indulge them. Gently return your mind to clear blue sky.

Inhale through your nose, puffing out your belly, exhale through the back of your throat.

"HER"

Inhale through your nose, puffing out your belly, exhale through the back of your throat.

"HER"

Inhale through your nose, puffing out your belly, exhale through the back of your throat.

"HER"

Inhale through your nose, puffing out your belly, exhale through the back of your throat.

"HER"

What we draw our attention to gets larger, your distractions can make you anxious, so for right now, we will only be observers of our thoughts as they drift across our clear blue sky. When we are finished we can constructively handle these concerns or tasks. For right now, we have our clear blue sky.

Inhale through your nose, puffing out your belly, exhale through the back of your throat.

"HER"

Inhale through your nose, puffing out your belly, exhale through the back of your throat.

"HER"

Inhale through your nose, puffing out your belly, exhale through the back of your throat.

"HER"

Inhale through your nose, puffing out your belly, exhale through the back of your throat.

"HER"

We are beginning to feel very relaxed as our mind is transformed from beta, our waking state to alpha, our meditation or light sleep state.

Inhale through your nose, puffing out your belly, exhale through the back of your throat.

"HER"

Inhale through your nose, puffing out your belly, exhale through the back of your throat.

"HER"

Inhale through your nose, puffing out your belly, exhale through the back of your throat.

"HER"

We are no longer paying attention to time or space and it is here where our power and intuition is present.

You will know this if a solution pops into your mind. Put it in that thought cloud and allow it to drift across your clear blue sky. You can come back to that later.

Inhale through your nose, puffing out your belly, exhale through the back of your throat.

"HER"

Inhale through your nose, puffing out your belly, exhale through the back of your throat.

"HER"

Inhale through your nose, puffing out your belly, exhale through the back of your throat.

"HER"

Know that when you clear your mind in this way, it opens the door for greater health and wisdom. Solutions often appear organically as we breathe. All the answers are within you. All the power is within you.

Inhale through your nose, puffing out your belly, exhale through the back of your throat.

"HER"

Inhale through your nose, puffing out your belly, exhale through the back of your throat.

"HER"

Inhale through your nose, puffing out your belly, exhale through the back of your throat.

"HER"

Clear blue sky.

Inhale through your nose, puffing out your belly, exhale through the back of your throat.

"HER"

Inhale through your nose, puffing out your belly, exhale through the back of your throat.

"HER"

Inhale through your nose, puffing out your belly, exhale through the back of your throat.

"HER"

With our last three breaths, we are going to conclude our directed relaxation session. Start to wiggle your fingers and toes. Now slowly open your eyes and return to the room.

APPENDIX B.
PERMISSION TO USE PANAS

Permission to use PANAS
From: Ja0000000@XXX
Sent: Tuesday, September 13, 2011 10:58 AM
To: Watson, D.
Subject: Permission Request

Hi Dr. Watson,

I am a doctoral student at Capella University and would like permission to use the PANAS in my dissertation. How would I go about this?

Thank you
Jayan M Landry

Subject: **RE: PANAS Permission**
Date: 9/13/2011 2:14:46 P.M. Eastern Daylight Time
From: david-watson@xxx.edu
To: Jayantip@xxx
CC: kthomas@xxx, la.clark@xxx, db.watson@xxx

Sent from the Internet (Details)

Dear Jayan,

I appreciate your interest in the Positive and Negative Affect Schedule (PANAS), and I am pleased to grant you permission to use the PANAS in your dissertation research. Please note that to use the PANAS, you need both our permission and the permission of the American Psychological Association (APA), which is the official copyright holder of the instrument. Because I am copying this email to APA, however, you do not have to request permission separately from APA; this single e-mail constitutes official approval from both parties.

We make the PANAS available without charge for non-commercial research purposes. We do require that all printed versions of the PANAS include a full citation and copyright information. Thus, any printed copies should state:

"From "Development and validation of brief measures of positive and negative affect: The PANAS scales," by D. Watson, L. A. Clark, and A. Tellegen, 1988, Journal of Personality and Social Psychology, 54, 1063-1070. Copyright © 1988 by the American Psychological Association. Reproduced with permission."

Please note that this permission does not include administering the PANAS online. If you are conducting a Web-based study, you should contact Karen Thomas at: kthomas@xxx.

Finally, Dr. Clark and I have relocated to the University of Notre Dame. Please direct any future correspondence to our new email addresses there (<u>la.clark@xxx</u>; <u>db.watson@xxx</u>).

Good luck with your dissertation.

Cordially,
David Watson

David Watson
Andrew J. McKenna Family Professor
Department of Psychology
118 Haggar Hall
University of Notre Dame
Notre Dame IN 46556

APPENDIX C.
THE PANAS SCALE AND SCORING
& DATA COLLECTION FORM

This scale consists of a number of words that describe different feelings and emotions. Read each item and then mark the appropriate answer in the space next to that word. Indicate <u>to what extent you generally feel this way</u>, that is, how you feel <u>on the average</u>. Use the following scale to record your answers:

1	2	3	4	5
very slightly	a little	moderately	quite a bit	extremely or not at all

____P____ interested	____N____ irritable
____N____ distressed	____P____ alert
____P____ excited	____N____ ashamed
____N____ upset	____P____ inspired
____P____ strong	____N____ nervous
____N____ guilty	____P____ determined
____N____ scared	____P____ attentive
____N____ hostile	____N____ jittery

_____P_____ enthusiastic	_____P_____ active
_____P_____ proud	_____N_____ afraid

P = Positive Affect item
N = Negative Affect item

[To score the PANAS, simply sum the responses to the 10 items comprising each scale.]

From Watson, D., Clark, L. A., & Tellegen, A. (1988). Development and validation of brief measures of positive and negative affect: The PANAS scales. Journal of Personality and Social Psychology, 54(6), 1063-1070. Copyright © 1988 by the American Psychological Association. Reproduced with permission. No further reproduction or distribution is permitted without written permission from the American Psychological.

DATA COLLECTION TOOL

Date		
Number		
Name		
Phone #		
Consent signed		
Unusual events? (Return Visit)		
Pre PANAS P-N		
PRE BP/Pulse		
12 min Bowl or Silence B/S		
Second BP/Pulse		
20 min DR		
Post BP/pulse		
Post Panas P-N		
Self report "Do you feel more relaxed than when we started?"		

APPENDIX D.
RECRUITMENT FLYER

RESEARCH BEING CONDUCTED

Are you interested in experiencing relaxation
techniques with a licensed mental health therapist?
If you take part in two free relaxation sessions, you may help
us have a better understanding about how people relax.
You will learn relaxation techniques in these
two free sessions and also contribute to research
on the topic of stress management.
There is no fee involved and both sessions will take
place over two weeks in a private therapy office at
Main Street, XXX, MA. Second floor. Sessions will
be conducted by Jayan Landry MS, ARNP, Licensed
Psychotherapist. Call now to schedule your appointment:
978. XXX.XXX.

APPENDIX E.
HSB TONE VERIFICATION

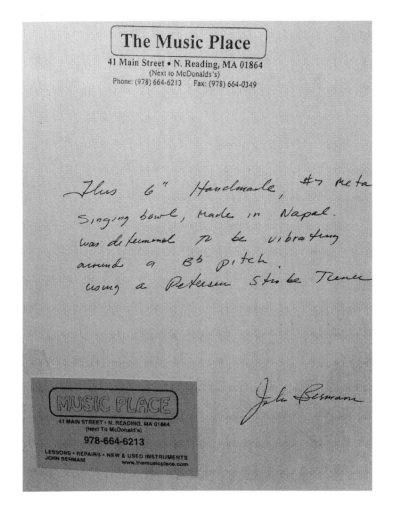

The Music Place

41 Main Street • N. Reading, MA 01864
(Next to McDonalds's)
Phone: (978) 664-6213   Fax: (978) 664-0349

This 6" Handmade, #7 Meta
Singing bowl, Made in Napal.
was determined to be vibrating
around a Bb pitch.
using a Peterson Strobe Tuner

John Berman

MUSIC PLACE

41 MAIN STREET • N. READING, MA 01864
(Next To McDonald's)
978-664-6213
LESSONS • REPAIRS • NEW & USED INSTRUMENTS
JOHN BERMANI   www.themusicplace.com

APPENDIX F.
INFORMED CONSENT FORM

Study Title: Measuring The Effects Of A Himalayan Singing Bowl On A Meditation Practice - A Quantitative Approach.

Researcher: Jayan Marie Landry MS, ARNP-BC

Email Address and Telephone Number: JayaXXXX@xxx Phone: 978.xxx.xxx

Research Supervisor: Dr. Thomas Page

Email Address: Thomas.page@xxx.xxx.

You are invited to be part of a research study. The researcher is a doctoral candidate at Capella University in the School of Counseling. The information in this form is provided to help you decide if you want to participate. The form describes what you will have to do during the study along with risks and benefits.

If you have any questions or do not understand this form, ask the researcher to clarify. Do not sign the consent unless the researcher has answered your questions and you decide you want to be part of this study.

WHAT IS THIS STUDY ABOUT?

The researcher wants to learn about your well-being and state of relaxation during a directed relaxation (DR) session.

The researcher also wants to know how people respond to sound during a relaxation session.

WHY AM I BEING ASKED TO BE IN THE STUDY?

You are invited to be in the study because you are an adult from the community who would like to add to the body of knowledge in the area of relaxation.

All participants will be 18 or over, with no age cap.

If you do not meet the description above, you are not able to be in the study.

HOW MANY PEOPLE WILL BE IN THIS STUDY?

About 50 participants will be in this study.

WHO IS PAYING FOR THIS STUDY?

The researcher is not receiving funds to conduct this study.

WILL IT COST ANYTHING TO BE IN THIS STUDY?

You do not have to pay to be in the study.

HOW LONG WILL I BE IN THE STUDY?

Jayan Marie Landry PhD

If you decide to be in this study, your participation will last about fifty minutes. You will go to Main Street Second floor, XXXXXX, MA, twice during a two-week period of time.

WHAT WILL HAPPEN DURING THIS STUDY?

If you decide to be in this study, and if you sign this form, you will do the following things:

Give personal information about yourself, such as your age and gender.

Answer questions during an interview about how relaxed you feel.

Complete a survey about positive and negative emotional states.

Allow a researcher to observe you while you relax during a pre-recorded directed meditation session.

Allow a researcher to look at your data collected during the sessions.

While you are in the study, you will be expected to:

Follow the instructions you are given.

Tell the researcher if you want to stop being in the study at any time.

WILL I BE RECORDED?

The researcher will not audio or videotape the sessions.

WILL THIS STUDY HELP ME?

Being in this study may not help you directly. Information from this study might help researchers help others in the future.

ARE THERE RISKS TO ME IF I AM IN THIS STUDY?

As part of the study, there will be an automatic blood pressure (BP) cuff applied to your arm to monitor your pulse and (BP). It is similar to what you may have experienced in your doctor's office and like in the doctor's office, you may feel slight tightness when the cuff is inflating for the series of three readings to be taken during your session.

You may stop being in the study at any time if you become uncomfortable.

WILL I GET PAID?

You will not receive any compensation for being in the study.

DO I HAVE TO BE IN THIS STUDY?

No - your participation in this study is voluntary. You can decide not to be in the study and can change your mind about being in the study at any time. There will be no penalty to you. If you want to discontinue study participation, tell the researcher.

The researcher can remove you from the study at any time. This could happen if:

The researcher believes it is best for you to stop being in the study.

You do not follow directions about the study.

You no longer meet the inclusion criteria to participate.

WHO WILL USE AND SHARE INFORMATION ABOUT MY BEING IN THIS STUDY?

Any information you provide in this study that could identify you such as your name, age, or other personal information will be kept confidential. Data will be collected with pen and paper on site at researcher's private practice office locked between sessions and after hours. Participants will be assigned a number. All materials related to research will be transported sealed to a totally secure location for tabulation. All results are tabulated in a password-protected computer or kept in a locked file cabinet. Only the researcher and Capella supervisor will be able to view this information. All results and materials collected will remain confidential. In any written reports or publications, no one will be able to identify you.

Limits of Privacy (Confidentiality)

Generally speaking, the researcher will keep session observations and data confidential. However, there may be instances when the researcher must share privileged information.

The researcher <u>cannot</u> keep things private (confidential) when:

The researcher finds out a child or vulnerable adult has been abused.

The researcher finds out a person plans to harm him or herself.

The researcher finds out a person plans to harm someone else.

There are laws requiring many professionals take action if they think a person might harm self, another, or if a child or adult is being abused. In addition, there are guidelines that researchers must follow to make sure all people are treated with respect and kept safe. In most states, there is a government agency that must be told if someone is being abused or plans to harm self or another person. Please ask any questions you may have about this issue before agreeing to be in the study. It is important you do not feel betrayed if it turns out the researcher cannot keep some things private.

WHO CAN I TALK TO ABOUT THIS STUDY?

You can ask questions about the study at any time. You can call the researcher if you have any concerns or complaints. You may call the researcher at the phone number listed on page one of this form if you have questions about the study procedures, study costs (none), study payment (none), or if you get hurt or sick during the study.

The Capella Research Integrity Office (RIO) has been established to protect the rights and welfare of human research participants. Please contact them at 1-888-XXX-XXX, for any of the following reasons:

You have questions about your rights as a research participant.

You wish to discuss problems or concerns.

You have suggestions to improve the participant experience.

You do not feel comfortable talking with the researcher.

You may contact the RIO without giving your name. Information you provide may be revealed in order to follow-up on a problem or concern reported.

DO YOU WANT TO BE IN THIS STUDY?

I have read this form, and I have been able to ask questions about this study. The researcher has talked with me about this study. The researcher has answered all my questions. I voluntarily agree to be in this study. I agree to allow the use and sharing of my study-related records as described above.

By signing this form, I have not given up any of my legal rights as a research participant. I will get a signed copy of this consent form for my records.

_____

Printed Name of Participant

_____   _____

Signature of Participant   Date

I attest that the participant named above had enough time to consider this information, had an opportunity to ask questions, and voluntarily agreed to be in this study.

_____

Printed name of Researcher

_____   _____

Signature of Researcher   Date

Capella IRB Approval

SECTION 3

PULLING IT ALL TOGETHER

SECTION THREE

CHAPTER 1

PULLING IT ALL TOGETHER

In Section 1, stress effects and management were covered in detail. Nine pearls of wisdom, cultivated from decades of experience working with survivors, were offered as tools for your emotional first aid toolbox in an effort to help you live your healthiest life. Section 2 encompassed my comprehensive doctoral dissertation on the effects of Himalayan singing bowl exposure formatted in proper research language. In this final section, the results gleaned from the dissertation will be summarized using a format similar to Section 1. It is my hope, by the end of our time together, you will have a thorough understanding of Himalayan singing bowl therapy HSB, and be well equipped and confident in your ability to implement the strategies offered.

Stress: The Upside

Stress offers many benefits, including sharpened focus, increased energy, and alertness for academic, business, or athletic performance. Stress is a critical component of the fight-or-flight reactions needed for survival. Most of us will be able to manage stress while maintaining optimal health.

Stress: The Downside—Rationale for the Study

Some of us will be overwhelmed by stress, which affects emotional and physical well-being. As a mental health practitioner, I wanted to determine HSB effects using an *empirical* approach to yield hard evidence describing these effects on our physiology. Empirical means the experiment results are derived from credible and objective observation rather than from someone else's ideas or imagination. Studies conducted empirically deliver results based on scientific proof, such as those gleaned from my dissertation.

Study Purpose: Answer Three Questions

The primary research question (one) and sub-questions (two and three) in the study shared in Section 2 are:

1. What are the physiological (blood pressure and heart rate) and relaxation effects (positive and negative affect states, also known as PANAS) when adding a Himalayan singing bowl HSB session just before a directed relaxation session?
2. Will the HSB produce an enhanced effect on blood pressure and heart rate when added prior to a directed relaxation DR session versus no HSB exposure prior to a meditation session?
3. Will there be an enhanced relaxation experience measuring positive and negative affect (PANAS) with HSB exposure prior to directed relaxation session as opposed to no HSB exposure prior to directed relaxation session?

Positive Affect States—interested, excited, strong, enthusiastic, proud, alert, inspired, determined, attentive, and active.

Negative Affect States—distressed, upset, guilty, scared, hostile, irritable, ashamed, nervous, jittery, and afraid.

PANAS is a tool proven to be effective in measuring the above affect states. The rationale for PANAS choice was detailed in the dissertation along with a copy of the instrument. Permission to use PANAS was obtained from the creator, Dr. David Watson, and his e-mail confirmation is also included in Section 2.

Study Blueprint

Before conducting an empirical research project, one must choose a study design, similar to a blueprint or road map, on how to proceed. There are three choices; the method I used is in bold print.

1. Qualitative
2. **Quantitative**
3. Mixed

Qualitative research investigates the *why* and *how* of decision making, not just *what, where,* and *when.* Usually much smaller sample sizes from one and up, using description with a specific focus, offer the researcher answers about how an intervention affects a few people.

Quantitative research calls for a larger sample size (thirty to thousands) and uses statistics, mathematical or numerical data, to answer questions about how an intervention affects *many* people. The greater the sample, the more you can rely on the results. Choosing this method for my study, fifty-one participants completed both meditation sessions, offering 102 data collection sessions. There were sixteen males and thirty-five females with an average age of forty-four, reflective of the town's population. This offered the numbers needed to provide an unbiased result, which can be generalized to a larger population. Quantitative methods can also be used to determine which *hypothesis* is true. Mixed research uses a combination of both qualitative and quantitative methods.

A *hypothesis* is an unproven theory, statement, proposition, or supposition.

A *directional hypothesis* is a statement of the specific nature (direction) of the relationship between two or more variables.

My directional hypothesis: There is a positive relationship between the use of HSB, resulting in enhanced relaxation and positive physiological effects, when used prior to a directed relaxation DR compared to no HSB prior to DR.

Study volunteers were recruited using proper research protocol with strict ethics. Details are found in Section 2. The participants completed two separate sessions within one month thereby serving as their own control. This allowed me to compare apples to apples with the same person. I used a coin flip to determine if they would have the twelve-minute HSB intervention first or the same twelve-minute time frame sitting alone in the office (silence intervention). The coin toss enabled me to avoid introducing a fixed variable and an ordering effect. In other words, the bowl versus the silence was randomly assigned, which offered greater validity to the results. The opposite intervention was used for the return session. Since "heads" was the bowl intervention, if that came up first, when they returned for session two, they sat in the office for those twelve minutes alone and in silence. If "tails" came up, they had the silence intervention first and on their second session, the bowl was used.

The same twenty-minute directed relaxation DR audio, offering a mindfulness breath and mind focus exercise, was played following both interventions. The entire directed relaxation script is found in this section. You may choose to record the script for yourself and play it back to create similar study conditions. Study volunteers completed the PANAS short-form questionnaire before and after each session. With all participants, the same blood pressure cuff (IntelliSense by Omron) was applied to the volunteer's same arm, automatically recording blood pressure and heart rate before the session, after twelve minutes of HSB or silence, and following the twenty-minute directed relaxation audio.

Blood pressure, heart rate, and PANAS scores were collected and later analyzed using Statistical Package for the Social Sciences (SPSS). SPSS software is widely used for statistical analysis in social science by education and health researchers, survey companies, and the government.

Using the same volunteer, blood pressure, heart rate, and PANAS were measured, comparing their HSB session with their silence session before the directed relaxation on session one and the return session two. Detailed tables and graphs showing the statistical results are in Section 2.

The Bottom Line on the Statistics

Results indicated there was a positive effect from HSB on blood pressure and heart rate, which lowered significantly over time in both groups. There was a statistically significant difference and change in systolic (top number) and diastolic (bottom number) blood pressure over time with the HSB having the greater decline compared to the silence intervention. Heart rate decreased in a similar pattern to blood pressure. The participant was considered hypertensive if he or she had a baseline systolic blood pressure over 140 mmHg on intake. There were twenty hypertensives, and surprisingly, that group had a statistically significant decrease with the HSB session. Both positive and negative PANAS scores fell significantly over time with greater decreases in negative scores in HSB over the silence group.

Statistically significant: In order to have useful results and draw conclusions, it's imperative to have enough data to properly represent the phenomenon or population being studied. A finding is called *statistically significant* if the probability of its occurrence, purely by chance, is less than one in twenty or (5 percent). If that is the case, the researcher can conclude that the observed effect actually reflects the characteristics of the population. The study yielded statistically significant results.

The hypertensive group responses offered unexpected findings with the study volunteers presenting with high blood pressure.

Referred to as "incidental hypertensives,"
this group had a statistically significant difference
in lowering their blood pressure after the HSB
session compared to the silence intervention.

Additional Interesting Responses

Fifty out of fifty-one participants reported feeling more relaxed at the end of both sessions, as indicated by positive associations with HSB exposure (deeper meditative state, enhanced spiritual experience, and ocean imagery). One participant reported feeling the same at the end of both sessions. Forty-eight out of fifty-one preferred the HSB to the silence session.

The following information describes participant responses after data collection on the final session, regarding HSB:

Soothing bowl sound: Three reported the bowl was more soothing than silence.

Bowl and relaxation: Thirty-three reported obtaining a deeper relaxed state with the bowl.

Sleep states: No participants reported falling asleep during the silence session. Three participants fell asleep during the directed relaxation segment of the silence session. During HSB, one participant reported feeling sleepy, with eight falling asleep during bowl playing as evidenced by snoring and/or presence of rapid eye movement sleep state with reporting of dreams during session. One of the eight fell asleep within the first two minutes of HSB as evidenced by snoring.

Involuntary body movements: When one participant fell asleep during bowl exposure, his right index finger moved involuntarily. Another participant noted her arms were *frozen in a good way.*

Church associations: Four participants had a positive association with church during the directed meditation, sensing God was present. One participant used guided imagery to walk through the woods to a chapel where she felt very peaceful and relaxed.

Spiritual: One participant traveled outside his body to another place describing it as a deeply spiritual experience; another stated she had the deepest past-life experience during bowl session.

Chakras: One participant reported accomplishing energy work in her crown chakra, while another described a tingling in that same chakra. A third described seeing the colors of purple and blue, associated with the crown chakra.

Changes in affect/mind states facilitating relaxation: The researcher made the decision to alternate bowl strike to bowl rub with both running out to silence based on review of literature regarding dynamics of bowl playing (detailed in Section 2, and in conversations with Mitch Nur, 2011 [32]). Most participants responded favorably to this method ($n = 49$) with two stating the strike segments brought them out of a deeper state where they were called to attention. The bowl rub was described as stimulating and calming at the same time, soothing, and sound trailing to silence very relaxing.

Participants noted greater focus and peace with HSB and described feeling the bowl through their whole body while enjoying the continuity of sound.

Other comments during HSB included:

- I felt beautiful, the energy came up through my feet causing deeper meditation.
- The bowl helped with internal focus on my body, I loved it.
- If I was lying down, I'd be asleep.
- I felt calmer, more chilled out, extreme serene.
- I felt like I was floating, and by giving me something to tune into helped me feel more focused.

- I was better able to concentrate, relax, and ignore my distracting thoughts.
- I was able to be more clear-minded, and when it was over, I felt like I was brought to another place offering greater peace.
- I felt dazed-in a good way, less stressed, and slower from the inside out.
- I could feel the vibrations of the bowl inside my body, which was more relaxed than my mind.

Associations with musicians: One participant was a drummer who attained a deeper relaxed state by tuning into the rhythm of the bowl; another, a pianist, related to the harmony of the bowl.

Imagery: Twelve participants reported attaining a deeper meditative state, which included imaginary trips to European mountaintops and Paris, along with vivid descriptions, such as "the wind was blowing through my hair, and I wanted to live in that peaceful state." Other images during bowl play included seeing clouds, feeling the bowl reverberate like the ocean, and traveling to the ocean where it was peaceful. One participant experienced the outside office traffic sounds turning into ocean waves that crashed on the beach, in unison with HSB rhythm.

Hypertensives: Three out of five known hypertensive participants who were taking antihypertensive medication had a diastolic blood pressure of 90 mm Hg at the end of the second session. Nine participants, who were not previously diagnosed, were hypertensive in the study through both sessions. All hypertensive participants were referred to their primary care physician for follow-up evaluation.

Bottom Line

Study results proved a positive relationship between exposure to Himalayan singing bowl HSB and physiological and relaxation responses when used prior to a directed relaxation session. The physiological differences were captured using statistical analysis that indicated statistically significant changes in systolic blood pressure and heart rate, with the HSB intervention in comparison to the silence intervention. In addition, HSB exposure has the potential to create a deeper meditative experience and decrease negative affect states.

There was a positive relationship between HSB exposure and physiological and relaxation responses as evidenced by significantly greater decline in systolic blood pressure and heart rate with HSB when compared to silence alone.

Future studies could be conducted using only participants with high blood pressure. The relaxation approach developed for this study could have positive ramifications for the hypertensive population.

The HSB technique can be an important part of self-care therapy for all. The art of playing the bowl is easy to learn, inexpensive, and carries no foreseeable risks. Adding the HSB to a meditation session increases the relaxation response, an important part of stress management. Stress management contributes to improve physical and mental well-being, which leads to a deeper quality of life.

By now, I hope you have come to the conclusion that setting aside time to incorporate a regular practice using my pearls of wisdom and considering HSB use, will add to the quality of your life. This final "Do It Yourself" book section will teach you how to purchase and play a HSB using the Landry Method.

The Landry Method is the bowl playing protocol I developed and utilized for my doctoral research study. It is an original and distinctive pattern of how to play the HSB and based on a thorough analysis of related research and consultation with experts in the field as described in Section 2. May your approach be—*progress not perfection,* when learning something new. Have fun and enjoy!

CHAPTER 2

LEARN TO PLAY THE HSB IN TWO STEPS

Step One: Obtain a Bowl and Puja

Consider purchasing a handmade Himalayan Singing Bowl HSB. The specific bowl used in this study is from Nepal and when rubbed and struck with the impacting stick, or puja, the six-inch circular metal HSB vibrated around a B^b pitch. It cost $150 in 2010. Bowls come in various sizes and shapes offering unique tones. When selecting your bowl, you can choose one similar to that used in the study. Or, you may wish to explore other bowl options. Keep in mind the most important variables include a pleasing tone to *you* and your ability to play it when struck or rimmed. A bowl of six-inches or smaller is a good starting place for beginners. Larger bowls have amazing sounds as well, but for the purpose of learning this method, the bowl needs to balance on the palm of your hand. That way you will get full benefit of the effects as the healing vibrations resonate up your arm and throughout your body when played.

The metal singing bowls are often ancient and come from different areas in the Himalayan mountain range, such as Tibet,

Bhutan, and Nepal. They are typically smooth inside and out, and have various dents and irregularities in the bowl walls (handmade). If there is a stamp, it may be faint and on the inside. Look for a sticker on the bottom that indicates where it was made. I have bowls from Nepal and have found them at; Circles of Wisdom in Andover, MA, Kripalu in Lenox, MA, and through Mitch Nur, http://www.9ways.org. In Rockport, MA, I had an amazing, energizing experience while standing barefoot in a gigantic, authentic Tibetan HSB. I was at the *Floating Lotus* when the bowl owner used a mega puja to rim the edge as vibrations engulfed my entire body from toes up to my head (floatinglotus.net). The calming effects seemed to last for a few hours after the memorable experience.

Machine-made bowls are much less expensive (twenty dollars and up, depending on size), and often have a heavy detailed pattern stamped into the bottom or around the edges. They are perfectly symmetrical and usually have no dents or dings. You may have more difficulty playing the bowl for they have a noticeable lack of continual ring tone. If you had a machine-made and an authentic bowl side by side, the most noticeable difference when striking would be the quality and length of the ring tone. The authentic handmade bowl will ring much longer than the machine-made bowl. With all this said, you may still wish to experiment with an inexpensive machine-made bowl and note the effects for yourself before making an investment in a handmade one. The goal is to get started on a new tool for your wellness program. Make decisions that are *right for you* at this time.

If your goal is to get as close to the results of this study as possible, an authentic HSB is recommended, due to its ability to ring the length of time needed for the Landry Method.

Puja: The puja is the stick needed to play the bowl and often comes with the purchase, at no additional cost. The larger the bowl, the larger the puja needed to make the bowl sing. The wooden puja, also known as the *exciting stick*, has one end wrapped in cotton and covered with soft leather. It is used to produce sound from the bowl by striking or rimming the bowl side or top edge. The idea is similar to making drinking glasses *sing*, by rimming your finger around the top edge. The puja takes the place of your finger along the top or side of the metal bowl.

Crystal bowls are also popular and may offer similar benefits. I find the sound and vibration of crystal bowls pleasing, but they can be fragile and are more likely to break. The metal bowls are strong, can take wear and tear, and travel easier than crystal. Since metal conducts heat, it's important to play your metal HSB at room temperature. You will experience greater ease at getting your bowl to *sing* as it warms over time with play.

Step Two: Get Familiar with Making Sounds

It helps to think of the bowl as an upside-down bell without a striker in the middle. You and your puja become the human striker to make the bowl hum, ring, or sing.

Begin by placing the bowl bottom onto the palm of your nondominant hand. With open palm, spread your fingers wide. Avoid touching the bowl sides, for this dampens the sound. See Photo 1.

Photo 1. Holding the Bowl

Hold the bowl with your palm up and fingers open.

In your dominant hand, hold the bare wooden end of the stick (puja) and begin rimming the outside of the bowl with the leather side of the puja. The challenge here is to balance and hold the bowl against the resistance you are creating with the puja. Think about pushing the puja against the bowl and the bowl against the puja at the same time. See Photos 2 and 3.

Photo 2. Using the Puja   *Photo 3*. Using the Puja

Rim the bowl with the puja.

If you are having trouble hearing the hum of the bowl, try softly striking the bowl with either end of the puja to get it started and then join into the ring with the puja by rimming the bowl until it begins to hum. It usually takes a little practice, but you will get the hang of it if you are patient and persistent. Some of my clients are able to make the bowl hum right away, others take a few sessions, but in all cases, I see a face that reflects a mixture of quiet joy and pride when he or she gets the bowl to sing.

Once you've mastered the art of making sounds happen with your bowl, you can experiment with finding your own pattern or use the one I developed, the Landry Method, used in the HSB research project described in Section 2. The next Chapter will fully explain the Landry Method offering you an easy step-by-step approach to playing HSB.

CHAPTER 3

THE LANDRY METHOD

If you have purchased or borrowed a HSB, you are ready to practice the Landry Method. This consists of two parts.

Part A: playing the HSB continuously for twelve minutes using a specific technique.

Part B: listening to the twenty-minute directed relaxation.

Part A: The HSB Technique

1. Carve out some quiet time in a comfortable location free of distractions. Plan on playing the bowl for a total of twelve minutes. At first, you may consider using a stopwatch or phone app to get accustomed to the timing and sequence of the Landry Method. Get comfortable in your seated position in a chair or on the couch. Use a pillow to cushion the arm holding the bowl. In your nondominant hand, hold the bowl, and with your dominant hand, hold the puja as described in step two.

2. Minute one. For the first minute, strike the bowl once with the leather side of the puja, and allow the sound to trail off for the next thirty seconds. Strike again once,

and let the sound trail for the remaining thirty seconds. This is your first minute. Do you notice as you begin to focus on the sound getting dimmer, you feel more calm and focused? It's okay if you don't—be patient and proud of yourself just for trying to learn something new.

3. Minute two. For the second minute, jump in on the trailing end of that last strike and begin to rim the outside upper edge of the bowl with the leather side of the puja just before you hear a chattering sound. Chattering happens when the bowl is overplayed, and you will know it when you hear it. To correct this, learn to move the puja more slowly as the bowl's humming or singing increases, or back off altogether and pull the stick away. Continue to rim the bowl slowly and back off as needed to avoid the chattering sound for the next minute. You will fall into a comfortable rhythm and pace for yourself.

4. Repeat minute one and minute two directions for the entire twelve minutes.

Bowl Goal: Try to keep the bowl sounds going during the entire twelve minutes. If it stops, that's okay. Strike the bowl to get it started and continue to play. Don't forget to have fun with it. You are offering this gift to yourself.

Part B: Directed Relaxation DR

In my research study, the same six-inch diameter HSB was played for twelve minutes as described in Part A. Immediately following, all study participants listened to the pre-recorded directed relaxation DR script, the partial version is found in dissertation Section 2.

Dr. Landry's directed relaxation script (below) represents the entire twenty-minute audio relaxation session used in the study. I recommend you read out loud and either record yourself, or choose your safe person with a calming voice to record it for you. Saving the audio script on your iPad, cell phone, or Dictaphone enables you to have easy access to your directed relaxation anytime you are in need.

Dr. Landry's Directed Relaxation Script

Get comfortable in your seated position moving your body and using the cushions to provide maximum support.

Know that when you take this time over the next twenty minutes to clear your mind, you will be helping your body and mind become more relaxed.

Being in this relaxed state is good for your body and mind.

Now if you are comfortable, close your eyes to minimize distractions and place your hands on your lower belly.

Picture breathing into your front and back lungs as you inhale through your nose. As you inhale, puff out your lower abdomen like a balloon, feeling your hands rise over your lower belly.

Inhale through your nose, puffing out your belly, exhale through the back of your throat and with your lips open make the sound "HEEEEEEEEER."

Inhale through your nose, puffing out your belly, exhale through the back of your throat and with your lips open make the sound "HEEEEEEEER."

Inhale through your nose, puffing out your belly, exhale through the back of your throat and with your lips open make the sound "HEEEEEEEER."

Inhale through your nose, puffing out your belly, exhale through the back of your throat and with your lips open make the sound "HEEEEEEEER."

Inhale through your nose, puffing out your belly, exhale through the back of your throat and with your lips open make the sound "HEEEEEEEER."

When you exhale, make the sound "her" with the back of your throat. Imagine trying to fog up a mirror held close to your lips. This is called ujjayi breathing or ocean sounding breath. Star Wars fans might call it the *Darth Vader Exhale*.

Inhale through your nose, puffing out your belly, exhale through the back of your throat and with your lips open make the sound "HEEEEEEEER."

Inhale through your nose, puffing out your belly, exhale through the back of your throat and with your lips open make the sound "HEEEEEEEER."

Inhale through your nose, puffing out your belly, exhale through the back of your throat and with your lips open make the sound "HEEEEEEEER."

Inhale through your nose, puffing out your belly, exhale through the back of your throat and with your lips open make the sound "HEEEEEEEEER."

Inhale through your nose, puffing out your belly, exhale through the back of your throat and with your lips open make the sound "HEEEEEEEEER."

When you breathe in this way, the "HEEEEEEEEER" sound stimulates the top of your 10th cranial nerve, innervating your parasympathetic nervous system. This nerve runs straight down from the throat through the center of your chest reducing your heart and respiratory rate along with calming stomach nerves.

The opposite happens when you are stressed. Breathing in this way helps relax your central nervous system eliciting branch two response. This is very helpful to your body and allows you to think more clearly.

Inhale through your nose, puffing out your belly, exhale through the back of your throat and with your lips open make the sound "HEEEEEEEEER."

Inhale through your nose, puffing out your belly, exhale through the back of your throat and with your lips open make the sound "HEEEEEEEEER."

Inhale through your nose, puffing out your belly, exhale through the back of your throat and with your lips open make the sound "HEEEEEEEEER."

Inhale through your nose, puffing out your belly, exhale through the back of your throat and with your lips open make the sound "HEEEEEEEEER."

Inhale through your nose, puffing out your belly, exhale through the back of your throat and with your lips open make the sound "HEEEEEEEEER."

And as you breathe in, picture a clear blue sky.

Inhale through your nose, puffing out your belly, exhale through the back of your throat and with your lips open make the sound "HEEEEEEEEER."

Inhale through your nose, puffing out your belly, exhale through the back of your throat and with your lips open make the sound "HEEEEEEEEER."

If a thought enters your mind, think of the thought as a cloud. Just be an observer of the cloud, and allow the wind to move the cloud across your clear blue sky and out of view.

Return to thinking about your clear blue sky.

Inhale through your nose, puffing out your belly, exhale through the back of your throat and with your lips open make the sound "HEEEEEEEEER."

Inhale through your nose, puffing out your belly, exhale through the back of your throat and with your lips open make the sound "HEEEEEEEEER."

Inhale through your nose, puffing out your belly, exhale through the back of your throat and with your lips open make the sound "HEEEEEEEER"

Inhale through your nose, puffing out your belly, exhale through the back of your throat and with your lips open make the sound "HEEEEEEEER."

Inhale through your nose, puffing out your belly, exhale through the back of your throat and with your lips open make the sound "HEEEEEEEER."

If any distracting thoughts enter your mind, do not indulge them. Gently return your mind to clear blue sky.

Inhale through your nose, puffing out your belly, exhale through the back of your throat and with your lips open make the sound "HEEEEEEEER."

Inhale through your nose, puffing out your belly, exhale through the back of your throat and with your lips open make the sound "HEEEEEEEER."

Inhale through your nose, puffing out your belly, exhale through the back of your throat and with your lips open make the sound "HEEEEEEEER."

Inhale through your nose, puffing out your belly, exhale through the back of your throat and with your lips open make the sound "HEEEEEEEER."

Inhale through your nose, puffing out your belly, exhale through the back of your throat and with your lips open make the sound "HEEEEEEEEER."

What you draw your attention to gets larger. Your distractions can make you anxious, so for right now, you will only be observers of your thoughts as they drift across your clear blue sky. Know when you are finished you can constructively handle these concerns or tasks. For right now, you have your clear blue sky.

Inhale through your nose, puffing out your belly, exhale through the back of your throat and with your lips open make the sound "HEEEEEEEEER."

Inhale through your nose, puffing out your belly, exhale through the back of your throat and with your lips open make the sound "HEEEEEEEEER."

Inhale through your nose, puffing out your belly, exhale through the back of your throat and with your lips open make the sound "HEEEEEEEEER."

Inhale through your nose, puffing out your belly, exhale through the back of your throat and with your lips open make the sound "HEEEEEEEEER."

Inhale through your nose, puffing out your belly, exhale through the back of your throat and with your lips open make the sound "HEEEEEEEEER."

You are beginning to feel very relaxed as your mind is transformed from beta, your waking state to alpha, your meditation or light sleep state.

Inhale through your nose, puffing out your belly, exhale through the back of your throat and with your lips open make the sound "HEEEEEEEEER."

Inhale through your nose, puffing out your belly, exhale through the back of your throat and with your lips open make the sound "HEEEEEEEEER."

Inhale through your nose, puffing out your belly, exhale through the back of your throat and with your lips open make the sound "HEEEEEEEEER."

Inhale through your nose, puffing out your belly, exhale through the back of your throat and with your lips open make the sound "HEEEEEEEEER."

Inhale through your nose, puffing out your belly, exhale through the back of your throat and with your lips open make the sound "HEEEEEEEEER."

You are no longer paying attention to time or space and here your power and intuition is present.

You will know this, if a solution enters your mind. Put it in the thought cloud and allow it to drift across your clear blue sky. You can come back to it later.

Jayan Marie Landry PhD

Inhale through your nose, puffing out your belly, exhale through the back of your throat and with your lips open make the sound "HEEEEEEEER."

Inhale through your nose, puffing out your belly, exhale through the back of your throat and with your lips open make the sound "HEEEEEEEER."

Inhale through your nose, puffing out your belly, exhale through the back of your throat and with your lips open make the sound "HEEEEEEEER."

Inhale through your nose, puffing out your belly, exhale through the back of your throat and with your lips open make the sound "HEEEEEEEER."

Inhale through your nose, puffing out your belly, exhale through the back of your throat and with your lips open make the sound "HEEEEEEEER."

Know that when you clear your mind in this way, it opens the door for greater health and wisdom. Solutions often appear organically as we breathe, for all the answers are within you. All the power is within you.

Inhale through your nose, puffing out your belly, exhale through the back of your throat and with your lips open make the sound "HEEEEEEEER."

Inhale through your nose, puffing out your belly, exhale through the back of your throat and with your lips open make the sound "HEEEEEEEER."

Inhale through your nose, puffing out your belly, exhale through the back of your throat and with your lips open make the sound "HEEEEEEEEER."

Inhale through your nose, puffing out your belly, exhale through the back of your throat and with your lips open make the sound "HEEEEEEEEER."

Inhale through your nose, puffing out your belly, exhale through the back of your throat and with your lips open make the sound "HEEEEEEEEER."

Clear— blue— sky.

Inhale through your nose, puffing out your belly, exhale through the back of your throat and with your lips open make the sound "HEEEEEEEEER."

Inhale through your nose, puffing out your belly, exhale through the back of your throat and with your lips open make the sound "HEEEEEEEEER."

Inhale through your nose, puffing out your belly, exhale through the back of your throat and with your lips open make the sound "HEEEEEEEEER."

Inhale through your nose, puffing out your belly, exhale through the back of your throat and with your lips open make the sound "HEEEEEEEEER."

Inhale through your nose, puffing out your belly, exhale through the back of your throat and with your lips open make the sound "HEEEEEEEEER."

With your last 3 breaths, you will start concluding your directed relaxation session. Begin to wiggle your fingers and toes. Now slowly open your eyes and return to the room.

That's all there is to it! If you practiced this exercise, observe how your body feels. Often clients describe more lightness in their head and chest. I often see shoulders relax and facial expressions soften. Take action and try using this tool just before going to sleep if you are struggling with insomnia. If you do this meditation daily for thirty days, you will begin to notice healthy differences in the way you feel.

AFTERWORD

In my private practice, I've had the privilege of working with clients seeking mental health support due to any number of issues including: grief, anxiety, trauma exposure and depressive disorders. When we begin assessing the areas of self-care and self-love, many stare blankly at me, as if they have just entered into unexplored terrain and I am speaking a foreign language. For so long, much of their lives revolved around children, significant others, and extended family. They honestly declare they have lost themselves along the way and don't even know what makes them happy or sad anymore. Drifting far from their true *self,* most have never taken the time to explore personal needs over their lifetime.

Moorjani's book *Dying To Be Me* (2012),[33] is a wonderful resource for those seeking encouragement in the area of authenticity and self-love as it relates to battling disease. She shares her story about how she healed from her four-year struggle with cancer by making decisions from a place of personal truth.

When we are caring for ourselves, and aware of our own magnificence, we can exercise forbearance. Forbearance enables us to let others be who they are as we drop the need to control them. We also will not allow others to control us. If you are struggling in this area of control, you may find the next section on codependency very helpful.

Codependency and People Pleasing

If one's primary sense of fulfillment is derived from doing for others first—at the expense of the self—the individual may be suffering from *codependency* or *people pleasing*. If your physical, spiritual, and emotional well is dry, you are not able to quench your own thirst, let alone that of others. This often manifests in anxiety or depressive symptoms. If you are feeling worn out from saying, "yes" to numerous requests, consider practicing a different response. Next time try, "let me think about that and get back to you in…." (a few hours, a day, or next week).

After reading this book, hopefully, you are more tuned into the guideposts in your body. If the request by another is triggering physical symptoms or an emotional response, it is best to wait until the thinking part of your brain is online before you commit to action. Even if you want to do what is being asked, the newly proposed response puts space between you and the request, while allowing you to ponder if it is doable in light of other commitments pulling on your time and energy. More importantly, it lets the other person know you are considering yourself in the equation. People will treat you, based on how you treat yourself.

Married or single mothers with children are usually the clients who struggle most with codependency and people pleasing. Taught their whole lives mothers are to be self*less*, by putting others' needs before their own, they think self-care is too self*ish*. Problems begin if they continue to ignore personal needs while running all around town to carpool, organize play dates, attend sporting events, all the while juggling multiple demands of home and work. If being a martyr is thrown in, they are suffering (or pretending to be suffering) greatly in an effort to gain sympathy, attention or praise. But since all behavior has meaning, paying attention to these early warning signs without judging is key. Pain is inevitable but suffering is optional.

Self-Help

If your codependency and people pleasing has evolved from a life affected by the addictions of others, there are a number of supportive resources. Books, therapists, and self-help groups such as those previously mentioned, are available and guided by knowledgeable professionals and peers in recovery. If you are dealing with substances or behavior addictions, Alcoholics Anonymous (AA) Overeaters Anonymous (OA), Sex and Love (SLAA), Gambling (GA) will assist in awareness and healing.

Celebrate Recovery (CR) is a Christian-based Biblical recovery program grounded in the Beatitudes. Initially founded by Pastor John Baker of Saddleback Church, CR is now offered in many locations across the United States as a ministry within the Christian church. The focus is on helping others with hurts, habits and hang-ups. I have yet to meet anyone who has not experienced at least one of those.

Reaching for help in an *active* way, allows the therapy journey to begin. Meeting dates, times, and locations for all the groups mentioned above are posted on Internet websites. There is no charge for this high-quality support.

Be Patient with Yourself and Manage Guilt

Keep in mind that as you are growing in awareness and making positive changes in your life, being gentle with yourself will aid in your progress. Healthy thoughts and behavior patterns take time. If negative self-talk is well engrained, and those harmful voices are replaying destructive messages in your mind, stop them. Often we use the words *should have* done this or *shouldn't have* done that when we are referring to past decisions or deeds. *Should* may be used on yourself or others to describe a past behavior or action, and it implies judgment. Should statements are not helpful for personal growth, and guilt is often not too far behind.

Dr. Phil once said, "guilt is a useless emotion, it's like rocking in a rocking chair-it gives you something to do but it doesn't get you anywhere." I basically agree if we are talking about the guilt that comes from self-flagellation, for it doesn't change the past or affect the future. If you made a bad choice in the past, try to understand it in the context of when it was made given the knowledge you had at that time. Hindsight is 20/20. You can vow to make a different choice with your current knowledge and awareness going forward.

We are not the same people now as we were even a few minutes ago. Those on the path to health and well-being are constantly learning and growing from things read, people we meet, and experiences we have. When you put yourself down or beat yourself up with your own stick, you drain precious energy needed to solve the life challenges that eventually come along. Self-punishment only serves to disempower. Forgiveness of the self is required first, before attempting the hard work of forgiving others who have harmed us. Both are healthy indicators of self-love in action.

Unconditional Love

Some are fortunate to have had the gift of unconditional love and positive regard in their lives, offering that blueprint for self-love. Crisis can force us to be out of sync with this blueprint and is often the powerful motivator for the journey back home to the self. For those who have never had this healthy model, seek guidance from a great therapist and groups like those mentioned.

If I do not learn how to love God and then myself, I actually *become selfish*, when I turn to other people or things to fill the empty void. Of course there are many times when one must put personal needs on hold to make sacrifices for children and family, especially during the early years of child rearing. I am suggesting that you consider *yourself* in the equation and seek ways to discover a healthy balance. You cannot give away what you do not possess.

Otherwise, if you slide into the martyr role and harden there, you may develop a crippling midlife depressive or anxiety disorder. Or you may stay in a harmful, dead marriage and join the ranks of the "married miserables" as your soul is slowly extinguished. Or you drift so far from your partner that divorce becomes the healthiest alternative to save your spirit and/or your life.

Asking For Needs And Taking Initiative

Be careful not to fall into the trap of expecting others to know and offer what you need, for everyone else is busy considering their own concerns. I often hear from clients in a marital therapy session, "We've been married for twenty years, he should know what I want for my birthday." That may be true for some, but for many, expecting others to read our minds, will prove frustrating. In addition, we often change our minds with shifting circumstances.

A better approach involves continuing the journey of self-awareness. From that place of greater understanding, you will know what you require in all circumstances. Learning how to clearly ask for what you need, in a given moment prevents confusion and frustration for all involved.

The fact that you chose to read this book is a wonderful indicator you are making efforts to aid in your healing journey. Learning how to add HSB therapy to your wellness toolbox and implementing my pearls of wisdom are like stepping on another brick in the path toward living your healthiest life. Inch by inch, one step at a time, you are moving in a positive direction toward loving yourself. That's all I could hope for.

Consulting The Inner Guide

When dealing with a complex situation if you are faced with having to make difficult decisions, instead of leading with just one organ, such as your feelings (heart), also consult your thoughts (head), *and* gut instincts (stomach). If you are in the midst of a discussion with someone and your stomach tightens or you feel anxiety, learn to pay close attention to that physical signal. If your sleep is suddenly compromised, use your journal, books, and spiritual resources to ask the hard questions.

Digging deep and reaching for help requires the presence of self-love. When I've been taken or allowed myself to get off track, I lose clarity and balance. When I am off track, it is more difficult to fulfill my life purpose with ease, and my body begins to moan and groan with a stomach or headache. These physical symptoms are powerful, red flag indicators, alerting me that I am not loving myself enough to protect against the current situations or relationships in my life.

If you are a recovering perfectionist, like myself, we understand when the bar is set too high for us, it is also too high for those we love. This strips the joy from living. While I'm not suggesting you become content doing a lousy job, instead, do your best with the resources you have and be satisfied. Do not compare yourself to others. This doesn't serve you well. There will always be those who have more or less than you do. Often heard in recovery programs across the nation: "I am enough, I have enough, I do enough." Truly. When I am not judging or comparing myself to others, I can see my failings as opportunities to grow. When viewed from this perspective, most past *mistakes* have been my greatest blessings as I continue learning how to love myself unconditionally each day.

Tapping into your inner guide is easier than you think. All you need to do is learn how to listen and nurture that essential and often small voice. Ask yourself and write the answers to these often difficult questions:

- What brings me joy?
- What causes me pain?
- What do I trust?
- Who has proven trustworthy?
- What or who makes me feel ...
  small?
  shamed?
  invisible?
- What or who causes my stomach to tighten?
- Where and with whom do I feel at peace?
- Where and with whom do I feel unconditionally loved and accepted?
- Who makes me feel like I can do nothing wrong?
- Who has had my back when the going gets rough?

- Are those I trust mentally, physically, and spiritually healthy, or are they changing in positive ways as they actively seek that path and take action toward greater awareness and health?

Summary

In my deepest core, I know God has allowed many painful challenges and put me on this earth for a purpose. I am grateful He loves me too much to leave me where I am. Beyond supporting and raising my family, that purpose has been to be a healer of the emotional wounds for myself then others. In the process of that powerful work, I've been blessed with the privilege of meeting other gifted healers who have supported my efforts to dig into and heal life's deepest wounds.

In closing this book three years from the time started, I thank additional dear friends and mentors who have walked with me on my journey to get closer to Jesus. Each prayer warrior has taught me important life lessons. Charles Heseltine, Priscilla Jennings, Beth Harrington, Chris Doherty (my current guitar teacher), Pastor Jim Ennis, Celebrate Recovery and Music group, along with Woman's Step Study members at Grace Chapel Lexington, MA—all have helped me gain additional clarity while balancing my own needs with those of others.

When I boil down all the advice and self-help books I have digested to date, a few simple truths are distilled:

Answers to the hardest questions are within me.
Physical symptoms are my cues to guide the way.
Tuning inward toward God to find, and then
follow my bliss, brings me the joy I seek.

My life is most abundant when I am making choices from a place of love and hope versus a place of fear. May self-love enveloped in self-care be a priority as you grow forward by tuning inward.

I am honored to have received permission to conclude with Joseph Campbell's complete quote from the Hero's Journey. His words have offered clear direction at critical times in my life. To me, Campbell's writings are like a lighthouse that shines the way forward when life's seas get turbulent. Like God, light is inspiring, dispels dark and guides us if we are headed for the rocks. God used my friend Brenda's life to deliver that personal message directly to my refrigerator door:

> When you follow your bliss, and by bliss I mean the *deep sense of being in it,* and doing what the *push* is out of your own existence—it may not be fun, but it's your bliss and there's bliss behind pain too. You follow that, and doors will open where there were no doors before, where you would not have thought there were going to be doors, and where there wouldn't be a door for anybody else. There's something about the integrity of a life. And the world moves in and helps. It really does.
>
> —Joseph Campbell[1]

Yes, the world moves in and helps, it really does. Blessings to each of you as you learn to love yourself and live out your healthiest life along your journey. May you find *your* bliss.

NOTES

1   Joseph Campbell. *The Hero's Journey.* (Novato: New World Library, 1990). Reprinted with permission of the Joseph Campbell Foundation, jcf.org.

2   Albert Einstein, "What I Believe," *The Forum* 84, no. 4 (October 1930), 193–194.

3   Joseph Mitchell Chapple, *Heart Throbs, Volume Two,* (Boston: Chapple Publishing Company, 1911), pp. ii, 1-2. Surprisingly, "What is Success" is attributed to "Anon." in the index.

4   Associated Press, "Baby survives birth in train toilet, fall on tracks." May 24, 1999. Reprinted with permission.

5   Viktor Frankl, *Man's Search for Meaning* (New York: Buccaneer Books, Inc., 1984).

6   John Milton, *Paradise Lost* (New York: Penguin Books, 2000).

7   Sonja Lyubomirsky, *The How of Happiness: A Scientific Approach to Getting the Life You Want* (New York: Penguin Press, 2007).

8   Dale Carnegie, *How to Stop Worrying and Start Living* (New York: Pocket Books. 1984).

9   Salvatore R. Maddi and Mindy Hightower, "Hardiness and Optimism as Expressed in Coping Patterns," *Consulting Psychology Journal* 51, no. 2 (Spring 1999): 95–106.

10   Salvatore R. Maddi, "The Personality Construct of Hardiness: Effects on Experiencing, Coping, and Strain," *Consulting Psychology Journal* 51, no. 2 (Spring 1999): 83–95.

11   Marcus Aurelius, *Meditations* (Dover Publications, Inc., 1997).

12   Eleanor H. Porter, *Pollyanna* (L. C. Page, 1913).

13   NIV Woman's Devotional Bible. Grand Rapids, MI: Zondervan, 1995.

14   A. T. Beck, *The Diagnosis and Management of Depression.* (Philadelphia: University of Pennsylvania Press, 1967).

15 David Burns, *Feeling Good: The New Mood Therapy* (New York: Harper Collins, 1999).

16 Daniel Amen, *Change Your Brain, Change Your Life* (New York: Three Rivers Press, 1998).

17 *101 Quotes and Sayings from Maya Angelou*, ed. Rhonda Buckley (2014), Kindle edition.

18 Jeffrey Wise, "Stealth Super-Powers," *Psychology Today* (November 1, 2012).

19 R. M. Sapolsky, *Why Zebras Don't Get Ulcers: Third Edition* (New York: Holt Publishing,1998).

20 Stephen Stahl, *Stahl's Illustrated Anxiety, Stress, and PTSD* (New York: Cambridge University Press, 2013).

21 Laurel Parnell, *Tapping In* (Louisville, CO: Sounds True, Inc., 2008).

22 Britta K. Hölzel, James Carmody, Mark Vangel, Christina Congleton, Sita M. Yerramsetti, Tim Gard, and Sara W. Lazar, "Mindfulness practice leads to increases in regional brain gray matter density," *Psychiatry Research: Neuroimaging* 191, no. 1 (2011): 36.

23 James Pennebaker and Janel D. Seagal, "Forming a Story: The Health Benefits of Narrative," *Journal of Clinical Psychology* 55, no. 10 (1999): 1243–1254.

24 C. Gilpin. *National Geographic Abraham Lincoln* (Washington DC: National Geographic Society, 2012).

25 Ann Voscamp, *One Thousand Gifts: A Dare to Live Fully Right Where You Are* (Grand Rapids, MI: Zondervan, 2010).

26 J. S. Odendaal and S. M. Lehmann, The role of phenylethylamine during positive human-dog interaction, *Acta Veterinaria Brno* 69 (2000): 183–8.

27 J. Virtues-Ortega and G. Buela-Casal, Psychophysiological effects of human-animal interaction: theoretical issues and long-term interaction effects. *Journal of Nervous and Mental Disease* 194, no. 1 (2006): 52–7.

28 E. J. Sobo et al., Canine visitation (pet) therapy: pilot data on decreases in child pain perception. *Journal of Holistic Nursing* 24, no. 1 (2006): 51–7.

29 K. M. Cole et al., Animal-assisted therapy in patients hospitalized with heart failure. *American Journal of Critical Care* 16, no. 6 (2007): 575–85.

30 JoAnne Sehr et al., "Family Pet Visitation," *American Journal of Nursing* 113, no. 12 (December 2013).

31 Elizabeth Lesser, *Broken Open: How Difficult Times Can Help Us Grow.* (New York: Random House Inc., 2004).

32   Mitch Nur, classes (2006). Retrieved from http://nineways.tripod. com/2005classeswithmitchnur/id11html.

33   Anita Moorjani, *Dying To Be Me; My Journey from Cancer to Near Death to True Healing.* (United States: Hay House, Inc., 2012).

ABOUT THE AUTHOR

As a healer, Dr. Jayan Marie Landry, a licensed psychotherapist, Clinical Nurse Specialist & Nurse Practitioner with a doctorate in counseling psychology, has thirty years experience specializing in crisis intervention. As the cofounder of the first East Coast Trauma Intervention Program of Merrimack Valley (TIP) in 1993, she has experience with over 22,000 child and adult victims of trauma. Numerous international travel and clinical trauma healing experiences allow her to blend Eastern & Western philosophies in her private practice, JourneyZend, L.L.C. located in downtown Andover. With a clinical focus on life wellness, and healing losses related to grief and trauma, she works with clients who have anxiety, depression, PTSD, grief, losses, and life transitions. With her interest in Eastern complementary and alternative therapy methods, she also practices REIKI III and EMDR (eye movement desensitization and reprocessing). Her three prior publications include coloring books to help adults and children grieve losses related to sudden death, suicide and sexual touching in her "Helping Healing Series." As a cum laude graduate of Boston College, she received the prestigious "Boston College Young Alumni Achievement Award" (1999). She has been honored with a great number of community accolades, including the Merrimack Valley regional newspaper, The Eagle-Tribune's "Woman of the Year Award" (1999).